Unsolicited ADVICE ©

FOR THE

HIGH SCHOOL GRADUATE

A PRACTICAL GUIDE FOR BECOMING INDEPENDENT

With Love!

LINDA & DOUG HAMILTON

A PRACTICAL GUIDE FOR BECOMING INDEPENDENT

ISBN: 979-8-9887138-9-0
Library of Congress Control Number: 2025906295
Cover design: Elena Novosyolov
Illustrations by: Arttu Snellman
Layout by: Kyriaki Sofocleous

Stories to Last Press

www.StoriestoLast.com
Oakland, CA

DEDICATION

For Ben and Max

We love you. We feel proud and lucky to have you in our lives. We love spending time with you. We love witnessing you live your lives and become increasingly independent. Thank you for inspiring this book and so much more!

TABLE OF CONTENTS

INTRODUCTION

CONGRATULATIONS ON YOUR HIGH SCHOOL GRADUATION!

You're moving into a new phase of life. You may be going off to start college or trade school or a new job, leaving your childhood home to create a new home of your own. You're becoming independent.

You've Got This!

In your new abode — and independence — you'll be learning more about who you are, how you want to live, who you want to interact with, what you want and don't want, and what you need and don't need. You'll gain more clarity on your priorities and values. And many of these priorities and values will change over time because you'll change, and the world will change around you.

Change Is Natural and Inevitable

This is an exciting phase of your life with great times ahead. There will also be ups and downs, issues, conflicts, and problems to solve. We've been there. That's why we created this book with the hope that it will be helpful as you get through the hard stuff and come out the other side feeling more confident and wiser.

Whether you'll be living in a dorm, an apartment, or a shared house, this book is here for you — filled with useful advice, hacks, and a little humor as you walk your path.

A Note About

Nothing is worse than unsolicited advice. Seriously, don't give unsolicited advice. Ask people first if they WANT suggestions. Only if they say yes, advise away!

So why is this series called Unsolicited Advice?

First of all, we thought it was funny. Also, in our experience, advice is easier to take when it comes with a bit of humor and plenty of love and at 18 years old, not from your parents! Thirdly, in a book, you decide what to read and what suggestions to use.

While launching our sons off to college, they sometimes needed guidance, and so did we. Everyone does. So, in this book we compiled what we found the most meaningful and useful from many sources: parents, recent college graduates, college students, and experts. The advice comes from real-life lessons, mistakes, and wins.

Just remember, though: When given suggestions for anything in your life, take what is useful and sensible for you, and discard the rest. That's our suggestion about suggestions.

This book was created for you, a guide to help you navigate your newfound independence. It covers the little things (like laundry hacks) and the big stuff (like navigating new relationships). We hope it is a resource you can turn to now — and in the years ahead!

Love, Linda & Doug

When I left home, my mother said, "Don't forget to write."

And I thought, "Well, that's unlikely. It's a basic skill, isn't it?"

Your NEW INDEPENDENCE!

Your Path Will Be Unique!

The path you take through life probably won't look like the one you thought you'd take — and it definitely won't look like anyone else's. And that's how it's meant to be! Ask for directions? Absolutely! You can learn a lot from the routes others have taken. But remember: The crossroads you encounter will ultimately lead you toward your own unique journey. Once you walk any path, it's yours. Embrace it. Here's how!

Practice the skills of independence. Start practicing independence before you leave home and continue once you're in your new place. Do your own laundry, cook your own meals, manage your budget, and try out basic home maintenance. Take care of your stuff, and work on your time management. Forming positive habits takes effort, but it pays off in satisfaction, time saved, and money well spent. Bonus: It's never too late to learn! (YouTube tutorials rock!)

Ask for help when you need it – offer help when you can.

This is seriously one of life's greatest lessons. If you feel vulnerable asking for help, it means you're showing true courage. Asking someone to help you takes strength. It's action in the face of uncertainty.

Set goals. Declaring what you want helps you achieve it. Define both short-term and long-term goals for yourself, whether it's personal development (e.g., going to the gym three times a week), building relationships (e.g., talking to one new person at a party), or pursuing career and education aspirations. Goals give you direction and motivation and help you recognize opportunities when they present themselves.

- **Academic:** What's one thing you want to achieve this week?
- **Social:** How will you connect with someone new?
- **Self-Care:** What can you do to recharge?

> **Small steps lead to big progress!**

Share your goals to create opportunities. Yes, it can feel scary at first. Not everyone will be supportive, but sharing your goals is worth the risk. Keeping your goals a secret limits the connections and support others can offer. You may be surprised by the sources that opportunities can come from. If you verbalize what you want to achieve, you're more likely to get it.

Discomfort won't kill you. You're going to face new situations and meet new people. It might feel scary, but step into the discomfort anyway. Just be kind to yourself — take breaks and reflect as needed. Positive action in the face of discomfort can increase confidence.

LOL

My neighbor knocked on my door at 3 a.m. Yes ... 3 a.m.!

Luckily, I was awake playing the drums!

Embrace independence. Remember to appreciate the freedom and autonomy that comes with independence — don't take it for granted.

THAT WAY

THIS WAY

Responsibility Is a GOOD Thing.
Taking ownership of your decisions and actions is empowering. Sure, you might make mistakes, but those missteps are opportunities to learn and grow.

Avoid the blame game.
Blaming others or "the system" doesn't change anything. More often than not, it just makes you feel helpless. Instead, seek to understand. Education is power. It's also useful to recognize what part you play in the situation. (Everyone has a part!) What decisions or actions can you take to improve the situation for yourself or others? Even small steps can make a difference.

What's the difference between ignorance and apathy?

I don't know, and I don't care.

PRO TIP

Your word is your bond. Simply put, do what you say you're going to do. Being dependable builds trust — both with others and within yourself. Honor the commitments you make, even if they are difficult or inconvenient. This also helps you learn whether or not to make those same commitments in the future. Words are cheap; it's our actions that show who we are.

If you have to change plans
(because it does happen), be direct and honest. White lies can come back and bite you in the ass.

Explore your passions.
Take time to discover what truly excites you. Try a bunch of different activities and then pursue those that bring you joy. (Legally!)

Stay flexible. Life rarely goes as planned. Be adaptable and open to change. Some of your best memories will come from moments that didn't go as expected!

BUILD RESILIENCE

Life is full of challenges and setbacks. Resilience helps you bounce back. Here are some ways to develop it:

Positive Outlook: Focus on what you can control and practice gratitude.

Optimism: Negative thoughts steal your energy while positive thoughts build energy. Setbacks are usually temporary, and you often learn something from them.

Problem-Solving: Break challenges into manageable steps. Brainstorm alternative approaches.

Social Support: Build a network of friends who have your back, family members who love you, and mentors who can steer you in positive directions. Ask for help when you need it.

Emotional Regulation: Practice deep breathing, mindfulness, or journaling to manage stress. You can't control others, but you can control what you do with your reactions to people or events. The famous "count to ten before acting" actually works most of the time.

Adaptability: Practice being flexible. Embrace uncertainty, keep your mind open, and look for alternate pathways forward.

Self-Care: Exercise, floss and brush, feed your engine solid fuel, and remember: sleep = sanity. You only get one body, and it's got to last a long time.

WRAP UP!

You might have to work through some things. But these skills will last you a lifetime. Welcome to your independence!

For more tips on goal setting, thoughts on independence, and more, go to UnsolicitedAdviceBooks.com.

Your NEW HOME

Welcome to your new home!

Whether you're in a one-room dorm, sharing a two-bedroom apartment, or a house, this is your space now — own it! You'll learn how to maintain it and share it with others. Let's take it one room at a time.

Your BEDROOM

Your bedroom is your sanctuary (or shared sanctuary).

Keeping it organized and aesthetically pleasing assures that you have a place to relax and de-stress. Here are some tips to make it cozy, functional, and reflective of you.

Start with the Basics

- **A comfortable bed.** Get a pillow and sheets that help you snooze. Good sleep is your best friend. If the mattress doesn't work for you, consider adding a topper (like memory foam).
- **A collapsible laundry hamper (and actually use it!).** Short on space? Consider getting an over-the-door hook to keep it on the inside of your closet.

PRO TIP

Make your bed every morning. It starts your day strong and ends it with a cozy reward. (You'd be surprised what a difference this makes to your mood!)

Maximize your space. There are great, inexpensive ways to get organized in your bedroom. Here are a few:

- **A Bedside Caddy:** Hangs off the bed to store phones, glasses, books, and chargers.
- **An Over-the-Door Organizer:** It's great for shoes, toiletries, or snacks.
- **A Folding Storage Ottoman:** Works as a seat, footrest, and storage container.
- **Loft Your Bed (If Possible) for Extra Space:** More storage underneath = fewer tripping hazards and more room for activities.

PERSONALIZE IT

Your bedroom (or space in the dorm) really becomes yours with a photo board or cozy decor that makes you happy. It doesn't have to cost a lot either. Here are some ideas. Just remember to stick to the dorm or landlord rules (like no nails in the walls or no open flames).

✔ **Fairy lights or LED strips:** You can create lighting options for different feels and avoid fluorescent lights.

✔ **Throw blankets and accent pillows:** Textiles soften the look of a room.

✔ **Aromatherapy spray** (check with your roommate first!). Good smells create a more pleasant and healthier atmosphere, with the potential to improve moods and reduce stress.

✔ **Fake candles:** That golden flicker can warm up a space and add a sense of luxury or romance safely!

✔ **Framed posters or discarded street signs:** Even an inexpensive frame can elevate whatever image is inside.

✔ **Cozy rugs or curtains:** They help make even harsh dorm lighting bearable and add style.

✔ **Tapestries or fabric wall hangings:** They add color and texture to boring walls.

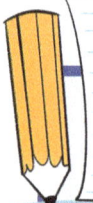

PRACTICAL MUST-HAVES

- ✔ A desk lamp
- ✔ Extra bed sheets
- ✔ Extension cords
- ✔ Surge protectors
- ✔ Multiport charging blocks
- ✔ A desk or clip-on fan.
- ✔ **Earplugs** for those nights when the party's next door or your roommate snores and your midterm is tomorrow.
- ✔ **Noise-canceling headphones are your best friend.** Your roommate's 2 a.m. TikTok binge doesn't have to be your problem.
- ✔ **A clip-on Desk Lamp** saves desk space, provides extra lighting, and can be used in bed too.

Have a "Do Not Disturb" signal. A door hanger, a certain playlist, or even a text — clear communication makes life smoother with fewer "interruptions."

Shower caddies aren't just for showers. They also make great snack holders, desk organizers, and even first-aid kits.

Label your snacks (or risk losing them). Unmarked snacks in a shared fridge are more likely to get poached because it is easier for the poacher to rationalize the deed. At the same time, don't eat food that is not yours, marked or unmarked. Food is a topic that people can react with more intensity than other items. Save you and them the grief.

PRO TIP

Keep your work space organized and separate from relaxation zones. It helps you focus and take real breaks.

LOL

When I was in college, my roommate used to clean my room, and I'd clean his.

We were maid for each other.

Be mindful of smells. If candles are banned, try Febreze, dryer sheets in drawers, aromatherapy sticks or diffusers, wax warmers, or plug-in air fresheners. And taking out the trash regularly is key...before it walks away on its own. And take showers!

LIFE HACKS!

A BETTER SMELLING BATHROOM

- **DIY Air Freshener:** Mix water, baking soda, and a few drops of essential oil in a spray bottle. Lavender or chamomile = instant relaxation.
- **Fresh Plants or Herbs:** Eucalyptus, lavender, and mint not only smell good but also purify the air.
- **Activated Charcoal or Baking Soda:** These absorb bad odors and can be placed in a small open container in your room. You can also sprinkle baking soda on your mattress, let it sit for an hour, and vacuum it up for a refresh.

FIRST CLASS BED MAKING

Follow these simple steps to make your bed as neat as a hotel bed. Bonus: No more cold feet sticking out of the blanket!

If you just use a duvet or comforter, tuck it in at the foot of the bed.

1. **Spread** out bottom, fitted sheet and fit corners of sheet around corners of mattress.

2. **Stand** at foot of bed and spread top sheet over fitted sheet. The end of the sheet with the large hem goes at head of bed. Leave a small space between top of sheet and head of bed.

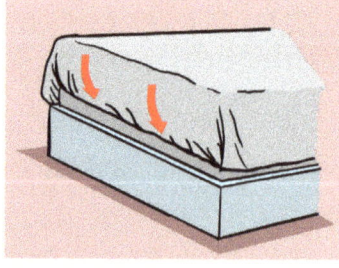

3. **At foot** of bed, tuck end of sheet between mattress and box springs. Ensure sheet lays smoothly between the two.

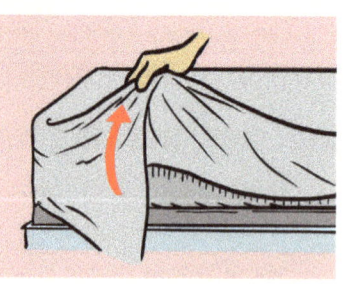

4. **Make** a hospital corner on one side of mattress of foot of bed. Grab and lift the draping sheet from the side about 16 inches from foot of bed.

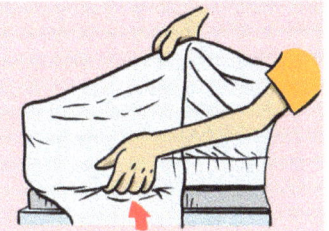

5. **Tuck in** triangle-shaped lower drape between mattress and box springs.

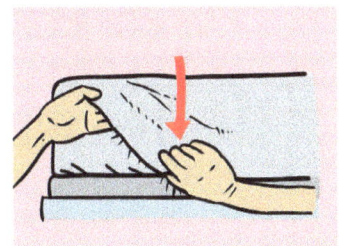

6. **Hold** the corner in place with your free hand and fold the top drape over. You want the fold on the top drape to form a 45-degree angle. Repeat on opposite corner of the mattress.

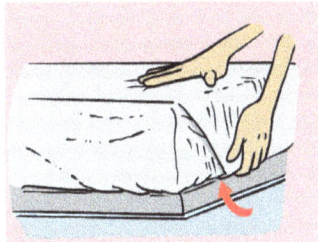

7. **Tuck in** sheet on both sides of the bed.

8. **Repeat** process with blanket. Put pillow in case and back on head of bed. Add comforter. Smooth everything down.

WRAP UP!

Your bedroom is your sanctuary. Make the time you spend there quality time.

For more bedroom hacks and decorative and practical tips, go to UnsolicitedAdviceBooks.com.

Your CLOSET & CLOTHING

Everything has a place.

Whether your storage is a cavernous walk-in closet or a tiny dorm nook, decide where everything "lives" and put it back after use. Read on for more tips to help you stay organized and always be able to find your stuff quickly.

Wallets/purses need a special spot where you always put them.

Avoid the stress of turning your room inside out to find your money, your ID, or your lip liner.

Keys need a home, too.

A hook near the door is a lifesaver. Set a record for consecutive days you put your keys in their designated spot. It will save you endless frustration and allow for instant departures.

"I'm just a disorganized person" isn't your forever story.

You can rewrite it by forming small habits over time. Patience, time, and a willingness to laugh at your messy moments will help build habits and keep friendships. You were a slob at home? Nobody needs to know.

Purge unused clothes now and then. If it doesn't "spark joy" (or fit), thank your pants or dress for its service and give it to a friend or donate it.

Leave space for the new. Don't bring every T-shirt or hoodie you own if you're in the dorms — campus life will load you up with free shirts from clubs, concerts, and events. You'll buy school swag, too!

Closet cleaning? Warning: Mess incoming! Pull everything out to sort. Donate what you don't need and organize as you put things back. The mess is temporary — order is coming!

Think of storage as a mini-mall. Designate part of a shelf in your closet for the pharmacy (medicine, tissues, vitamins). Designate another specific shelf space for your hardware store (nails, tools, pushpins). Another space is your office/student supply store (pens, paper, notebooks). Yet another is your sporting goods store (balls, racquets, mitts). This categorization makes organizing (and finding things) easy. Clean up on aisle nine!

Upgrade your hangers. Wire hangers are the villains of closets. They can create creases in your clothes where you don't want them, and shirts are more likely to slip off the hanger. Switch to slim velvet hangers — they're space-saving, nonslip, and won't make your clothes sad and droopy (thicker plastic hangers also work).

PRO TIP

The "just do it" rule. Always put stuff back where it belongs after use. Too tired? We feel you — but make time to clean up ASAP. Most chores take seconds or minutes. Prove it to yourself by timing them.

Clothes piles happen. Whether it's a post-party rush or midterm chaos, piles are normal. Just don't let them become permanent. Dealing with them now saves time (and sanity) later.

LOL

Why did the lion hide in my closet?

He said it was Narnia business.

Costume parties? Thrift it. Theme parties are a college staple, and thrift stores are your best friend for cheap, fun finds (different from "vintage" stores that charge too much for the same clothing).

KONMARI FOLDING ROCKS

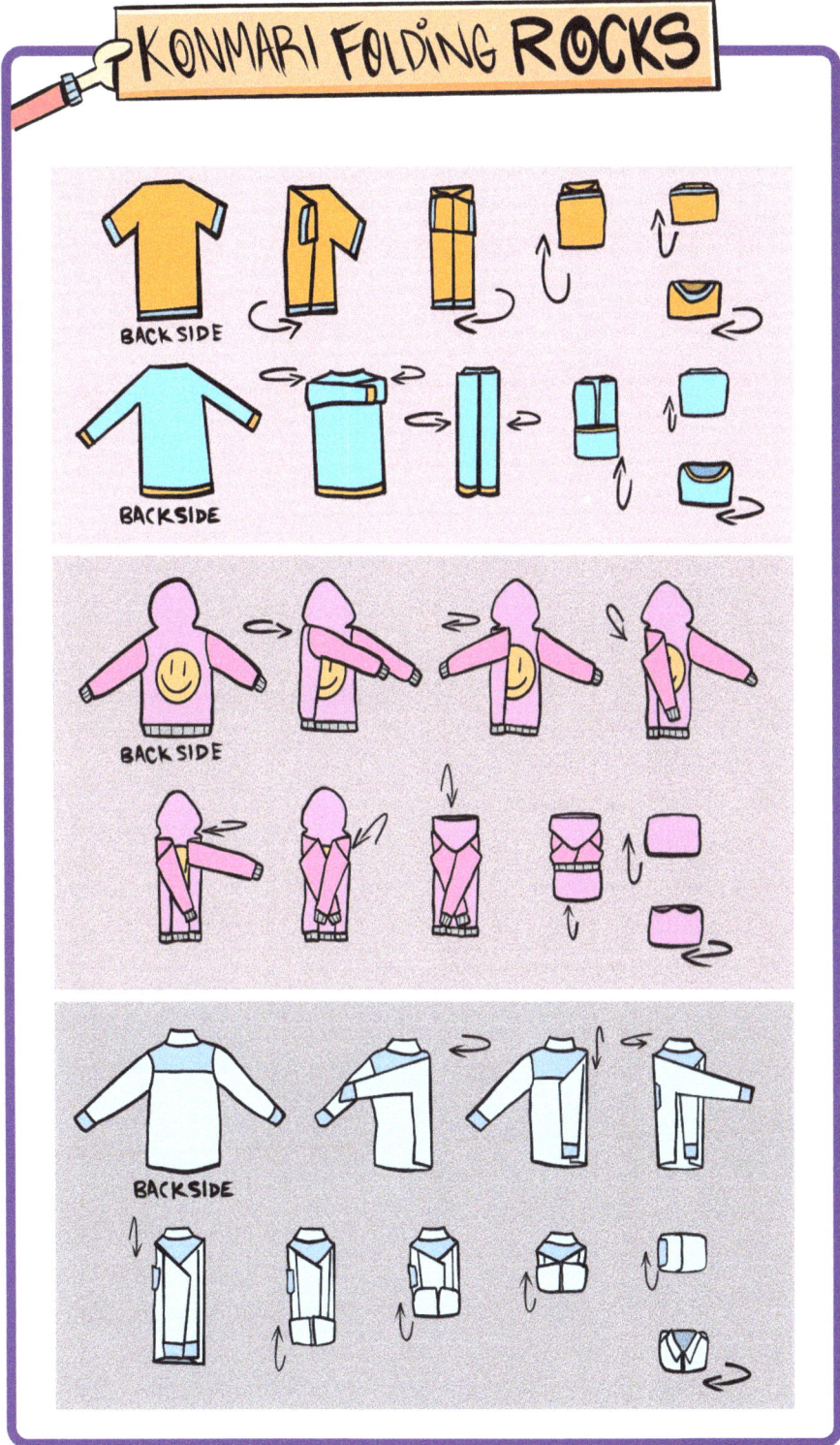

Keep one pair of dress shoes. Black or brown works, but black is more versatile. Even jeans can level up with nice shoes. This will save you time, storage space, and money. Parents in town? Dress shoes are a one-minute way to look better when they arrive.

Make sure you have "just in case" outfits. Have one "dinner party" look and one professional outfit ready to go. Whether it's a last-minute interview or a formal event, you'll be prepared.

Don't overstuff your closet. Smushed clothes = wrinkles. Keep it breathable by folding, rolling, or hanging with care (less is more). Realistically, we all have about fifteen favorite items that we wear most of the time.

Seasonal swaps save space. Plan to switch out your wardrobe once or twice a year. Bulky winter sweaters aren't helpful in spring, and sandals just take up room in winter.

Consider investing in a vacuum pump and storage bags for your off-season wear. You can get both for about $25.

WRAP UP!

Your closet doesn't have to be a black hole of chaos! Only keep what you love and actually wear, do quick cleanouts every few months, and don't let laundry pile up like a monster in the corner. A little effort now means less stress later — and more time to focus on the fun stuff — like actually getting dressed and heading out the door!

For more closet hacks, printable folding instructions, and more, visit UnsolicitedAdviceBooks.com.

Your BATHROOM

There's nothing like a clean, well-stocked space to set your mind at ease.

Especially when you're doing your business in the bathroom! This is where you go to get clean, but it's also the spot that can get the stinkiest and messiest in a flash. The key is to set up habits and routines (either solo or with roommates) to keep this space fresh and functional.

Respect the Bathroom Golden Rule. Always leave the bathroom cleaner than you found it — even in a public or shared bathroom. Wipe down the toilet seat, give it a quick scrub with a toilet brush, and don't leave those soap slivers in the shower! You're making the world a better place — one wipe at a time. Two words: air freshener.

Everything in Your Bathroom Needs Its Place. Decide where everything lives in your bathroom. Do you need additional shelves or storage bins? Create specific homes for your items to keep things from piling up in chaotic piles of toothpaste, razors, and spare shampoo bottles. Or hair from your brush getting into your toothbrush!

Toiletries are personal – some things are shareable, and some are not. Set clear boundaries and communicate them kindly with your roommates. If you need to borrow something in an emergency (shampoo, toothpaste, etc.), be upfront about it. Remember, honesty > secrets.

Here's the Key Toilet Paper Rule. Replace the empty roll every time and remind your roommates to do the same! Few things will cause more ill will than sitting down to realize you're out of TP. Make sure you've got extra rolls within arm's reach.

Don't Leave Your Ladies Hanging. If you have a communal box of tampons and pads in your dorm or house and you see supplies are running low, let your roomies know and buy more right away.

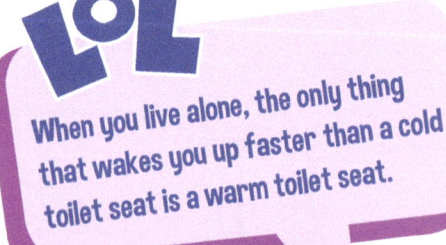

When you live alone, the only thing that wakes you up faster than a cold toilet seat is a warm toilet seat.

PRO TIP

Keep air freshener next to or on the back of the toilet. Use it before and after you go #2. A little spritz can mask those "earthy" smells, save embarrassment, and keep your bathroom accessible to your guests. Take a small container with you when traveling with others.

Towel Etiquette Makes a Difference. Hang towels neatly, not crumpled in a heap. A well-hung towel dries faster, looks better, stays fresher longer, and helps you avoid a messy bathroom.

TOWEL FOLDS FOR THE WIN

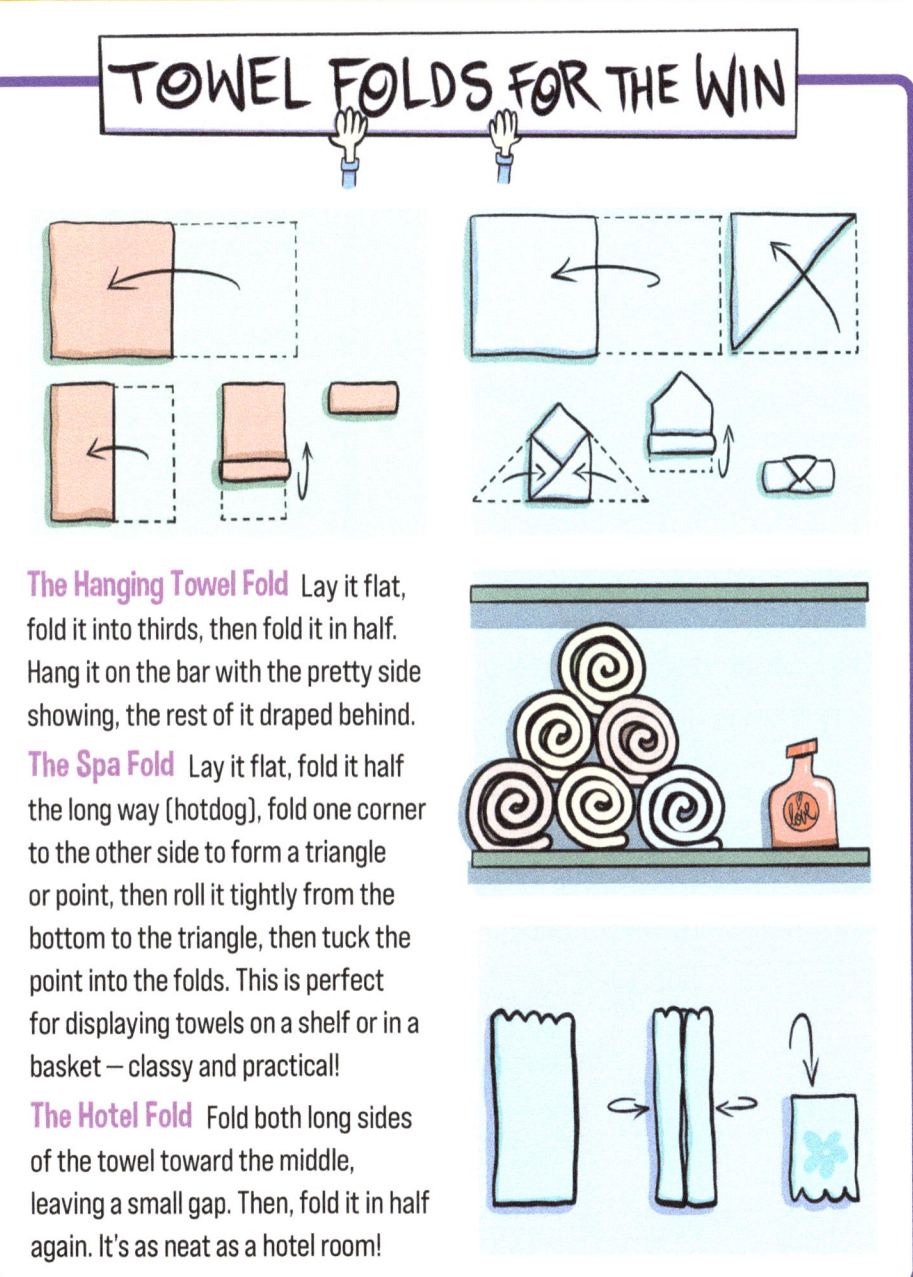

The Hanging Towel Fold Lay it flat, fold it into thirds, then fold it in half. Hang it on the bar with the pretty side showing, the rest of it draped behind.

The Spa Fold Lay it flat, fold it half the long way (hotdog), fold one corner to the other side to form a triangle or point, then roll it tightly from the bottom to the triangle, then tuck the point into the folds. This is perfect for displaying towels on a shelf or in a basket — classy and practical!

The Hotel Fold Fold both long sides of the towel toward the middle, leaving a small gap. Then, fold it in half again. It's as neat as a hotel room!

Cleaning the bathroom includes the shower. Scrub the floor, walls, and tiles — mold and mildew can grow between the grout lines and get gross fast. Trust us, you don't want that, especially if you have a quick gag reflex.

Try hair catchers. Put them over the drain in the shower to avoid a clog catastrophe.

Bathroom knowledge is power! Know how to use a plunger, and — here's a big one — how to turn off the toilet water supply. Few things ruin your day faster than an overflowing toilet.

Pre-strung flossers do the trick. Want to floss daily without putting your hands in your mouth? Pre-strung flossers are the way to go, and they come in biodegradable versions to cut down on microplastics in landfills.

Keep your hairbrush in a drawer or toiletry kit. If it's on the counter, it may become the community brush. Keep a small backup brush stashed elsewhere for emergencies.

Skin care is essential for everyone. Every bathroom needs a solid facial cleanser and moisturizer. No matter what your skin type, washing your face morning and night with the right product will keep your skin in check. Avoid harsh soaps — your face deserves better!

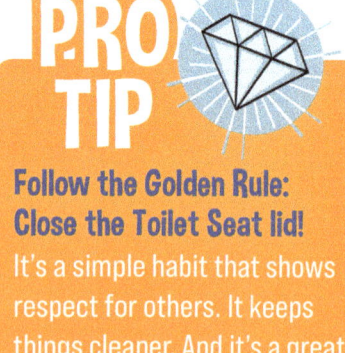

PRO TIP

Follow the Golden Rule: Close the Toilet Seat lid! It's a simple habit that shows respect for others. It keeps things cleaner. And it's a great lifetime habit that others appreciate.

CLEANING TOOLS YOU'LL ACTUALLY USE

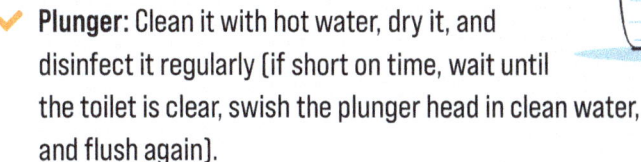

- ✔ **Plunger:** Clean it with hot water, dry it, and disinfect it regularly (if short on time, wait until the toilet is clear, swish the plunger head in clean water, and flush again).
- ✔ **Scrub Brush:** Keep it in a caddy for convenience and to keep it sanitary.
- ✔ **Toilet Cleaner:** Choose a disinfectant with stain-fighting and germ-killing properties.
- ✔ **All-Purpose Cleaner:** For soap scum, grime, and general bathroom yuck.
- ✔ **Glass Cleaner:** For streak-free, sparkling mirrors.
- ✔ **Microfiber Cloths or Paper Towels:** Use for wiping down surfaces, mirrors, and counters. Bonus: microfiber is eco-friendly.
- ✔ **Rubber Gloves (Optional):** Protect your hands from harsh chemicals. A good pair of waterproof gloves can save your skin (literally).

Ventilation Is Key. Open the window or turn on the exhaust fan while cleaning. It helps prevent mold and mildew.

Wash Your Hands! Seriously, wash them a lot — before and after eating. It's the key to staying healthy and avoiding acne.

Wash your towels. Wash them often, including hand towels. They can get musty and smelly fast.

LIFE HACKS!

- **Use vinegar to clean your showerhead.** Attach a plastic bag filled with vinegar over your showerhead and soak overnight to remove mineral deposits. It'll restore the water flow like magic.
- **Shoe organizers can work in the bathroom too.** Use one to store cleaning supplies or toiletries. Hang it on the back of a bathroom door for maximum space efficiency.
- **Try natural odor-reducing hacks.**
  - **Citrus fruits:** Place citrus peels or slices in a bowl for a natural and refreshing scent.
  - **Baking soda:** Place a bowl of baking soda in the bathroom to absorb odors.
  - **White vinegar:** Pour white vinegar in a bowl to absorb odors, especially musty smells.

Equip your bathroom with a diffuser or fragrant candle. For you and your guests, your time in the john will be a more pleasant experience.

PRO TIP

Keep a small broom and dustpan handy to sweep up hair and debris. If you want to level up, a handheld vacuum works wonders for quick cleanup.

WRAP UP!

And that's a wrap on the bathroom tips. Keep it clean, keep it organized, and remember to always be considerate (especially with that toilet seat). You've got this!

For more bathroom cleaning and decorating tips and recommended products, go to UnsolicitedAdviceBooks.com.

Your
LAUNDRY ROOM

Some simple actions in the laundry room will help your clothes last longer and look better.

But, as with all new habits, give yourself a grace period to get the habit into your routine. These tips will save you time and money as well as help you look mighty fine.

Check all pockets before washing. This is worth the extra time! It will save you from the horrors of gum on your favorite sweater, lip balm disasters, ink stains on your jeans, and potentially destroying precious receipts or air pods.

Wash new colorful clothes separately. At least the first couple of times. That vibrant new tie-dye has the potential to turn your white shirt into a blotchy pink shirt.

Tie any strings before washing. On sweatshirts, pants, or swimsuits, tie those strings into a tight bow. If that string does escape, you may be looking at an Olympic event trying to thread it back in.

LIFE HACKS!

You can restring it. If your hoodie string does come out, here's a life-saving hack: Spear the end of the string on a safety pin, push it through the passageway like an inchworm, and keep going until it pops out the other side.

Stock up on stain remover (hello, Spray-n-Wash!). Keep it near your washer or take it along to the laundromat. Spilled something? Spray it on the clothing stain a few minutes before washing. This may save your favorite shirt or skirt.

Bleach your whites periodically. Fill your washer halfway with warm water (cold for shrinkables), add soap and bleach, and let it soak for 15 minutes before continuing the cycle. Keep your whites looking bright, like your future.

PRO TIP

Tie a massive knot at both ends to ensure sweatshirt strings never escape again. #NoStringsLeftBehind

PRO TIP

Hard-to-Get-Out Stain Tip: For hard-to-get-out stains, spray them with stain remover and let them sit for an hour or even overnight, and reapply the spray to spots still remaining. This works pretty well on underarm stains on white shirts.

Clean out the lint drawer of your dryer before every load. If you ignore it, your dryer may not dry your clothes nearly as quickly. This can get expensive if you have quarter driven dryers.

STAIN REMOVAL GUIDE

- ✔ **Blood:** Soak in cold water, not hot. Dab with two tablespoons of ammonia for a few minutes and soak again. If light-colored, you can also dab it with hydrogen peroxide.
- ✔ **Coffee/Tea:** Remove the excess. Rinse with cold water. Rub in with liquid detergent. Sit for 5 minutes, then soak for 15 minutes. Spritz with a 50/50 vinegar-water mix. Rinse again with cold water.
- ✔ **Ink:** Dab a little non-gel toothpaste on the stain. Rub in and then wash off. Repeat if necessary. Alternative: Dab with rubbing alcohol and blot with a paper towel.
- ✔ **Mud:** Allow mud to dry completely. Using dish soap, rub with your fingers on both sides of the fabric and repeat. Wash as recommended.
- ✔ **Perspiration:** Create a paste with baking soda and water and apply it to the stain. Let it sit for an hour, then wash it in warm water if the fabric allows. Also, try 50/50 hydrogen peroxide and water and let it sit for 30 minutes.
- ✔ **Red Wine:** When wet right after the spill, dab with a clean cloth, do not rub. Create a paste with baking soda and water. Let it sit for an hour, then wash it in warm water if the fabric allows.
- ✔ **Sauces:** Remove excess and flush the stain from the back. Apply white vinegar directly to the stain and wash immediately.

Don't overfill the washer. It's tempting because who wants to spend more time (or money) washing clothes? But if you overstuff the machine, your clothes probably won't get as clean. Plus, it might damage the machine. Wash a smaller load for better results.

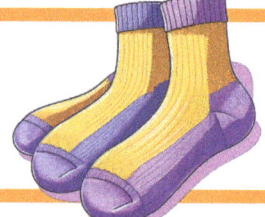

Keep your matching socks together in each wash load, maybe even with a rubber band.
Somewhere, there's a mountain of left-footed socks!

Give each item a quick shake before putting it in the dryer.
This will help your clothes dry faster with fewer wrinkles.

Use a dryer sheet with each dryer load. Your clothes will smell that much fresher.

WHEN TO USE COLD vs. HOT WATER TO WASH CLOTHES

✔ **Cold Water**
- Delicate fabrics (silk, wool, lace)
- Bright colors (no bleeding or fading)
- Stains (because hot water can set some stains)
- Energy efficiency (because saving money is always in style)
- Cotton and materials that can shrink (keep the sizing)

✔ **Hot Water**
- Heavy soiling (goodbye, grime!)
- White fabrics (because gray is not white)
- Towels and bedding (get them clean and sanitized)
- Allergy concerns (bye-bye dust mites!)
- Older T-shirts and clothing with color (the dyes are set by now — low risk of color bleeding)

Fold your clothes right out of the dryer.
If you let them sit in the hamper, they'll get wrinkled and lose that fresh-from-the-dryer smell. Soon, they will look like your dirty clothes, and you'll have to use the smell test. Bonus: No ironing necessary.

COMMUNAL LAUNDRY ROOM

Strategically pick your laundry times. The worst time to do laundry is when you've run out of clean underwear and you're in full panic mode. The best times are usually weekday afternoons or Friday/Saturday nights — but every campus is different, so get a feel for it.

Sort your laundry before you head to the laundry room. Use mesh bags or recycled grocery bags to separate whites and colors or delicates and regular wash items. Then you're ready to snag the first available washer.

Label your hamper, detergent, and dryer sheet box with your name and phone number. It's a lifesaver if you need to leave your laundry unattended. It might also save your clothes from ending up on the floor in a wet pile or your supplies claimed as community property.

Inspect the machines before using them. Seriously, check inside! You never know if someone left a rogue pen or lipstick that dropped out of a pocket during the cycle. If you find a problem, either clean it yourself or notify the laundry room manager.

Track your laundry times. How long does it take for your washer and dryer to do their thing? You'll thank yourself when you don't have to wait forever. Set an alarm so you don't forget! Others will be grateful if you take your clothes out of the dryer in a timely fashion, and your clothes won't sit out in a pile getting wrinkled.

Why are poker players good at doing laundry?

Because they know when to fold 'em! Ba-dum-tss!

Turn shirts/hoodies with decals or printed logos inside out before washing. This will help protect those graphics and prolong the life of your favorites.

Take dry clean-only items to the cleaners. Don't take chances with them in the washing machine. They probably won't wash well and it could even ruin them.

LAUNDRY SUPPLIES

Items That Can Seriously Up Your Laundry Game

- ✔ **Wash Clothes in Mesh Bags:** They protect delicate items like bras and undies from getting torn or tangled. Oh, and they keep socks together, too.
- ✔ **Storable Drying Rack:** Line-drying keeps your clothes in better shape. Get one that folds up so it's easy to store.
- ✔ **Stain Remover Pen:** Your best friend in the laundry room. Spills don't stand a chance!
- ✔ **Detergent Pods:** Light, easy, and no mess. Plus, they save you from lugging around heavy detergent bottles.
- ✔ **Mini-Steamer:** Skip the ironing board and keep your clothes looking pressed without the hassle.
- ✔ **Dryer Sheets:** Not only do they reduce static, but they also freshen up your shoes (goodbye, stinky sneakers!).

WRAP UP!

With these tips, you'll not only save time, money, and effort but also look fabulous. And you'll be a laundry pro. So, go forth and conquer in clean, wrinkle-free clothes!

For more laundry tips and handy printable guides, go to UnsolicitedAdviceBooks.com.

Your KITCHEN

There's nothing like a clean, well-stocked kitchen

when you're hungry and want to cook a meal quickly! Here are some tips to make your kitchen more enjoyable, even if it's just a mini-fridge or the place where you stash your snacks and drinks.

While cooking, clean as you go. Rinse pans right after use and put away ingredients as you go along. You'll have less to clean up when you're done eating and more time to get to the next task or make it to class on time.

Establish clear rules for kitchen use. This includes cleanliness, shared resources, and etiquette. Post these guidelines in the kitchen as a reminder for everyone. (If you find yourself saying, "I'm letting them soak," make sure that isn't short for "I don't want to do my dishes.")

Invest in sharp knives. A quality, sharp knife makes chopping and slicing easier and faster. Keep your knives well-maintained for maximum efficiency in the kitchen.

> Always smell the milk before you pour it on your cereal!

Chop safely. When chopping vegetables, curl your fingers inward to reduce the risk of cuts. If you do cut yourself, stop, disinfect, and bandage immediately. Less chance of infection and… less blood in the food!

Wipe down countertops *daily*. After food prep and at the end of the evening, wipe down surfaces. It cuts down on odors and food residue and prevents infestations of ants or rodents. Plus, it makes the kitchen a more pleasant place to hang out — the party's in the kitchen!

Keep your kitchen organized.
Store items and put them back in the same place every time. Designate specific areas for utensils, plates, and cooking accessories so you'll never waste time searching for them. The same goes for the fridge!

Label kitchen drawers and shelves. This makes it easier for everyone to put things away and remember where they are. Also, your friends may help you with the dishes and will know where to put them.

PRO TIP

Label and date your food. This prevents confusion about what belongs to whom and helps reduce food spoilage or waste. Designate shelves for each roommate and consider a shared shelf for communal food items. Don't eat someone's food without permission!

Implement a regular cleaning schedule. Assign cleaning tasks to yourself and your roommates or create a rotating schedule. This ensures the kitchen stays clean and hygienic for everyone. Task rotation cuts down on boredom, and no one gets stuck with the chore they hate for long.

Stock shared supplies. Keep dish soap, sponges, paper towels, and trash bags well-stocked. All participating roommates contribute to these purchases, or you all establish a small fund to cover the cost.

Close cupboards and drawers after use. Some people have the habit of leaving cupboards wide open as if a poltergeist haunted the kitchen. Not only does this look unkempt, but it can also lead to accidental head smacks.

Refrigerate perishables promptly. Wrap and seal food, then refrigerate it. Look up the best storage methods for different items to keep them fresh. Do not let any meat, fish, or cheese go into the fridge unwrapped.

Freeze bulk food to last. If you make a lot of pasta sauce or only use a quarter of a store-bought jar, freeze it, and it won't go bad if you eat it a week later. You can also pre-make meals to save prep time during the week. Just microwave and enjoy!

Store leftovers in airtight containers. Leftovers will last longer, taste better, and retain their consistency if stored properly. Check the fridge regularly so you don't forget they are there. (Potential for a smelly science project!)

Establish a system for reporting maintenance issues.
Keep a notepad on the fridge for things that need fixing — like broken appliances or plumbing problems. Be sure to address these issues quickly, and if renting, stay on top of reminders to the landlord (same-day reminders recommended).

Rinse dishes before loading them into the dishwasher. Pre-rinsing prevents food bits from clogging the filters and helps extend the life of your washer while increasing the cleanliness of your dishes.

Got an ant problem? Bug spray alone won't do the trick. You also need to step up your cleaning game to keep them away. They will stop coming if there's nothing to attract them.

Rat or mouse droppings? Put out traps immediately. If left unchecked, rodents can multiply quickly, damaging your property and gnawing through wires. Use peanut butter, bread, or sandwich meat as bait, and opt for catch-and-release traps when possible. (Mice and rats give birth every 19–20 days. Rats can have litters of 6–20 babies.) Do not use poison. Rats may die in the walls and smell, or you introduce poison into the local ecosystem ... like your cat.

STOCK YOUR SPICE RACK

A well-stocked spice rack can greatly enhance your cooking by adding depth and flavor. Here's a list of essential spices to keep on hand:

Salt: Essential for seasoning and enhancing the flavor of almost any dish.

Black Pepper: Adds warmth and depth to savory dishes.

Garlic Powder: A convenient way to add garlic flavor without using fresh garlic.

Onion Powder: A savory addition that works when fresh onions aren't available.

Paprika: Adds color and mild flavor; try sweet, smoked, or hot varieties.

Cumin: Earthy and nutty, commonly used in Mexican, Indian, African, and Middle Eastern dishes.

Chili Powder: Adds heat and flavor, especially to chili, soups, and stews.

Cayenne Pepper: A spicy kick for any dish — common to Cajun dishes — use sparingly!

Oregano: Robust and slightly bitter, great for Mediterranean and Italian cuisines.

Basil: A sweet, slightly peppery flavor, key to Italian cooking.

Thyme: Earthy and floral, it pairs well with poultry, vegetables, and soups.

Rosemary: Adds a pine-like aroma, perfect for roasted meats and veggies.

Bay Leaves: A subtle herbal flavor for soups and stews.

Cinnamon: Warmth and sweetness for both sweet and savory dishes.

Ground Ginger: Slightly spicy, perfect for Asian, Indian, and Middle Eastern dishes.

Nutmeg: Sweet and warm, great in baking and creamy sauces.

Ground Coriander: Citrus-like, often used in Indian and Mexican cuisines.

Turmeric: Earthy, vibrant, and widely used in Indian and Middle Eastern dishes.

Parsley: Fresh and peppery, a great garnish or flavoring in sauces and salads.

Red Pepper Flakes: Adds heat to dishes, commonly used in Italian, Mediterranean, and Asian recipes.

Elevate any eating experience by serving the food on a charcuterie board.

Arrange the food beautifully on a cutting board, butcher block, or platter. Use small bowls for nuts and sauces. Consider adorning it with flowers or herbs. You can do this for brunches, hors d'oeuvres, main meals, and desserts.

LOL

My roommates get mad when I steal their kitchen utensils.

But it's a whisk I'm willing to take.

Host community kitchen events.
Make dinner together or announce happy hours to bond with your roommates. Agree that everyone sets up and cleans up at these communal events.

LIFE HACKS!

- **Lemon for Microwave Cleaning:** Cut a lemon in half, squeeze the juice into a bowl of water, and microwave it for a few minutes. The steam loosens food splatters, making it easier to wipe clean.
- **Rubber Bands for Jar Grip:** Wrap a rubber band around the lid of a stubborn jar for extra grip when opening it.
- **Preventing a Pasta Boil-Over:** Put a wooden spoon across the top of the pan while boiling pasta, and the bubbling water will not overflow the pot.

WRAP UP!

These tips will help you keep a smooth-running kitchen that's also a great place to hang out.

For storage tips for specific foods, kitchen chore charts, more hacks, and even recipes, visit UnsolicitedAdviceBooks.com.

Your LIVING ROOM /SHARED SPACE

Your living room is the heart of the house!

Whether you're catching up with friends, watching a movie, or just hanging out, keeping this space cozy and clutter-free is key. If you're in a one-room dorm, this still counts — your room is your living room, too! Here are some ideas for making your living room space awesome.

Declutter & clean often.

It's easy for things to pile up — remote controls, laundry, snack crumbs, plates, and cups. Take a minute each day to tidy up. A clean floor and a clean couch will increase your relaxation factor.

Clean under the couch cushions.
It's shocking what you'll find — change, food bits, missing remotes, maybe even your lost homework. Don't skip this step! Every two weeks should cover it.

Arrange the furniture.
Think about how people move around the room and where conversations flow best. Create seating that encourages interaction and doesn't block paths. Quick test: Try running from room to room, and where you run into stuff or have to make sharp turns, adjust those angles for easier movement/flow.

Add some sound.
A soundbar for your TV can make a world of difference for movie nights, game-day parties, or noisy roommates.

Storage solutions.
Books, magazines, and random things like empty cans can pile up fast. Find a home for everything and stick to it — less clutter, more space.

Bring in nature.
Incorporating natural elements such as houseplants, wood furniture, or stone accents adds a sense of tranquility. Just make sure everyone's on board with watering duties!

Make it cozy.
Add comfortable seating, soft lighting, and decorative touches — whatever makes the space feel inviting. Encourage your roommates to chip in with personal touches.

Set quiet hours. If you have roommates with different schedules, set some "quiet time" rules for the living room. Everyone will appreciate the consideration.

Create the hangout spot. Want people to come to your place? Set up activities — movie nights, board games, DIY craft sessions, dance parties, or whatever makes you and your friends happy. If you build it, they will come!

Steam clean carpets. A deep clean every so often makes a big difference. Rent or buy a steam cleaner to make carpets look and smell fresh.

Vacuum under furniture. Don't forget those hard-to-reach spots! A handheld vacuum or crevice tool will do the trick. (If you don't do it, the cockroaches will.)

LIFE HACKS!

- **Dryer Sheets for Dusting:** Wipe baseboards with dryer sheets to keep dust at bay.
- **Lint Roller for Furniture:** Pet hair? Dust? Grab a lint roller for a quick fix on couches and chairs.
- **Ice Cubes for Carpet Dents:** Got dents in the carpet from furniture? Put ice cubes on them, let them melt, then fluff the fibers with a fork.
- **Microfiber Cloths for Dusting:** These little guys trap dust like magic. Use them on coffee tables, electronics, and shelves. On average, 50 percent of household dust is dead skin cells (Do you really want to breathe that?), so dusting is worth doing.
- **Vinegar for Glass:** Mix equal parts water and vinegar in a spray bottle, and you've got a streak-free glass cleaner.
- **Baking Soda for Odors:** Sprinkle baking soda on furniture or rugs, leave it for a few hours, and vacuum it up to freshen things up.

Create the vibe – lighting makes all the difference.

Soft, warm lighting creates a cozy atmosphere. Use string lights, floor lamps, or even candles to add ambiance.

Create zones for different activities.

If you have the space, divide your living room into small "zones." Create a cozy conversation area with chairs and cushions, a movie-watching space with comfy seating, and maybe a corner for games or puzzles. This will keep everyone from feeling cramped and allow different activities to flow.

Add a music station.

Set up a place to play music easily — whether it's a Bluetooth speaker, record player and stereo system. Create playlists based on the mood of the event (be careful who you share your AUX with).

Freshen the air with scents.

Bring in a pleasant smell with candles, diffusers, or essential oils. Choose soothing scents like lavender for relaxing or citrus for an energizing vibe. The right scent can make the space feel more welcoming.

Use cozy textiles.

Add throw blankets, oversized pillows, or even floor cushions for extra comfort. People love to curl up for movies or deep conversations. Plus, cozy textiles make the space feel inviting.

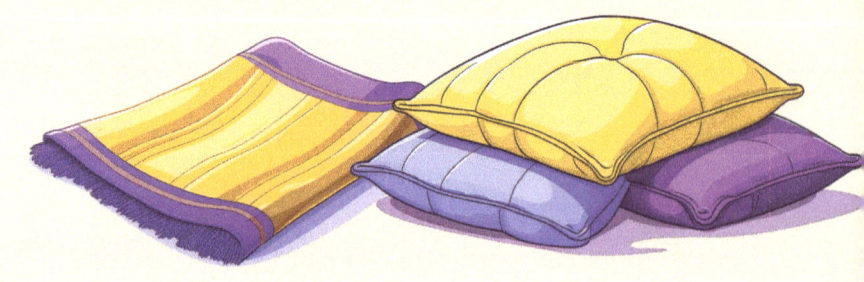

Use personal touches.

Show off your personality and the personalities of your roommates. Have a fun art display, like a chalkboard wall for messages or inspirational quotes. Or put up photos of places you've visited or your favorite moments. (Polaroid board for instant gratification — commemorate your visitors!)

Use comfortable and flexible seating.

Have a mix of seating — couches, chairs, floor pillows, and even beanbags. This gives people the freedom to move around and find their preferred spot. For more casual events, floor seating is perfect for lounging and socializing. (Keep a stack of folding chairs close by for sudden crowds.)

Create a snack and drink bar.

Create a designated snack station where guests can grab food and drinks easily. You could set up a popcorn machine, a candy bar, or a drink station with fun-themed drinks for your event.

Set up a puzzle table.

Set up a card table in a corner off to the side and put a 500-piece puzzle on the table. Gives people a place to collect themselves without leaving the group. Puzzles are surprisingly addictive and community-building.

LOL

Q: What's a clean house a sure sign of?

A: The internet is down!

Themed Movie Nights

Choose a theme — 80s classics, horror, or rom-coms — and get cozy. Make it a potluck or themed snack night. You could even hand out "movie tickets" to make it feel official. Don't forget comfy blankets! (Extreme Challenge: Hold a Star Wars Marathon — all eleven movies — 24 hours and 54 minutes of screen time!)

Game Night Galore

Bring out the board games, card games, and party games like Pictionary or charades. Or try a video game tournament if you're into that. Set up a "game station" for people to rotate through.

DIY Craft Party

Set up a crafting corner with supplies for making something simple, like custom T-shirts, friendship bracelets, sketchbooks, or painting mini-canvases. It's a creative way to spend time together, and you get to take something home as a souvenir. (Guests like this way more than they think they will!)

Indoor Picnic

Lay down a blanket, set up some pillows, and have a relaxed indoor picnic with sandwiches, fruit, and your favorite drinks. Bonus points if you play relaxing music or nature sounds in the background.

Karaoke Party

Find a karaoke app or sing along to YouTube karaoke videos. Add categories like duets, decades, movie and TV classics, genres, or lip-syncing performances to make the party even more dynamic. Consider purchasing a wireless Bluetooth karaoke mic (between $20–$30).

DIY Coffeehouse/Tea Party

Brew up a pot of coffee or tea, make a selection of pastries, and set up a little "menu." Set up the living room like a cozy café. Invite some local musicians to perform if you want to take it up a notch!

Trivia Night

Host a trivia night with categories like pop culture, history, music, or random facts. Create your own questions or use a trivia app for added ease. Playing in teams is usually the most fun. The team with the most correct answers wins a prize!

DIY Mystery Night

Set up a "who-done-it" mystery game where guests can play detective to figure out a fun crime. You can buy kits online or create your own simple plot. (Look up Murder Wink party game on Google.)

Outdoor Movie Night (If You Have a Balcony or Outdoor Space)

If you have a balcony, backyard, or just a projector, set up an outdoor movie night using a hanging sheet or wall as a big screen. Lay out blankets and lawn chairs and offer popcorn. Use a Bluetooth speaker to amplify the sound.

Potluck Dinner or International Cuisine Party

Have a potluck where everyone brings their favorite dish. You could take it a step further and make it an international cuisine night.

By adding simple, thoughtful touches, you can make your living room the ultimate space for hangouts, keep roommates happy, and keep your friends coming back for more good times!

To get your fung shui on and for more comfy living room and party ideas, including detailed printable instructions, go to UnsolicitedAdviceBooks.com.

Your DINING ROOM

Old-world manners? Totally still in!

Not only do they impress on dates or when meeting your roommate's parents, but they can also turn an ordinary meal into something special. A little effort in how you set the table can elevate your dinner game in a big way. Don't have a dining room? The tips in this section still apply. An attractive presentation of a meal makes it more memorable!

SETTING THE TABLE LIKE A BOSS

Here's a simple guide to setting a formal table that'll make you look like a pro, even if it's just pizza night.

Don't have a dining room? Using these tips, you can make even a fold-out table special for a night! Inside or outside.

Tablecloth or Placemats: Start by protecting your table and adding a little style with a tablecloth or placemat. It's like giving your meal a first-class seat.

Dinner Plate: Place your plate in the center of each place setting, about an inch from the edge of the table. Give it some space to breathe.

Napkin: Fold it up and place it either to the left of the plate or on top. (Bonus points for fancy folds or napkin rings.)

Fork: Position your fork to the left of the plate. If it's a multicourse dinner, smaller forks are for the salad or starter and are placed to the left of the larger fork which is used for the main course.

Knife: Place the knife to the right of the plate, with the blade facing in. If it's a multicourse affair, the smaller knife goes outside, and the larger knife stays close to the plate for the main dish.

Spoon: The spoon goes to the right of the knife.

Dessert Spoon & Fork (Optional): If dessert is on the menu, place the spoon and fork horizontally above the plate. Spoon near the plate, fork on top. This is like the Ritz!

Water Glass: Place it above the knife and slightly to the right. Hydration and classiness combined.

Wine Glass (Optional): Arrange your stemware above and to the right of the water glass. Red wine glasses go to the right of the white, if you're serving both.

Bread Plate & Butter Knife (Optional): If bread is involved, place the bread plate to the upper left of the dinner plate and the butter knife diagonally across it.

Play ambient music at a meal. Soft, mellow tunes in the background add an instantly classy vibe. Think jazz or acoustic or even classical.

EASY PEASY CHICKPEA CURRY

You don't need a culinary degree or a fridge full of ingredients to eat well. This warm, cozy chickpea curry costs less than a drive-thru meal, and it makes leftovers!

WHAT YOU NEED:

- 1 tablespoon oil (olive or whatever you've got)
- 1 small onion, chopped
- 2 garlic cloves, minced (or ½ tsp garlic powder if you're shortcutting)
- 1 can chickpeas (15 oz), drained & rinsed
- 1 can diced tomatoes (15 oz)
- ½ cup coconut milk (from a can or carton)
- 1 teaspoon curry powder
- ½ teaspoon cumin (optional but good)
- Salt & pepper to taste
- A squeeze of lime or lemon (optional but zesty)
- A handful of spinach or kale (fresh or frozen)

Total for the pot: around $4.00

Cost per serving (makes 3): about $1.33

HOW TO MAKE IT:

1. Heat oil in a pan over medium heat. Add the chopped onion and cook until soft (about 5 minutes).
2. Add garlic, curry powder, and cumin. Stir for 1 minute.
3. Add chickpeas, tomatoes, and coconut milk. Stir and simmer for 10–15 minutes.
4. Stir in greens near the end. Add salt, pepper, and citrus juice to taste.

WHAT TO SERVE WITH IT:

Spoon it over cooked rice or quinoa, or scoop it up with store-bought naan. Add a side of veggies, steamed or sauteed in a pan with salt and pepper.

 **LIFE HACKS!**

TABLECLOTH ALTERNATIVE HACKS

 **1.** **A Large Scarf or Shawl:** Use it as a runner right down the center. Adds a cozy, boho vibe to any table setup.

2. **Brown Kraft Paper or Butcher Paper:** Perfect for a casual look and doubles as a doodle-friendly surface for notes or games.

 3. **Newspaper or Magazines:** A quirky, artsy option that's also budget-friendly.

 **4.** **Gift Wrap:** Lay them flat and piece them together for a creative, eco-friendly look.

PRO TIP

You can serve any beverage in a wine glass, and it will elevate the experience. I'll drink to that!

WRAP UP!

With these simple tricks, you'll make your dining room — or makeshift dining room — feel special, whether you're serving a home-cooked meal or just ordering takeout! Bon appétit!

For more fun dining table decor, dinner party ideas, and charcuterie ideas, including detailed printable instructions, go to UnsolicitedAdviceBooks.com.

Your THINGS

We live in a world of stuff!

Things tend to pile up — quickly. You can save time, money, space, and a lot of headaches in the future by learning to be mindful of what you own, what you need, and what you want. Here are some suggestions about your stuff.

Everything you own requires something from you. It needs to be cleaned, stored, repaired, updated, or maintained. Before bringing something new into your life, ask yourself, "Do I have the time and energy to take care of this thing?"

WHY LESS IS MORE

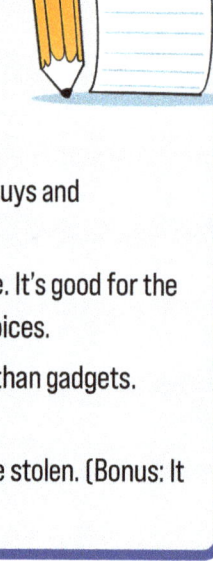

People are choosing to own less for all kinds of reasons:

✔ **Simplicity:** Less stuff = less stress. A decluttered space makes life easier and keeps you focused on what matters.

✔ **Financial Freedom:** You'll save money by avoiding impulse buys and prioritizing quality over quantity.

✔ **Environmental Impact:** Fewer possessions mean less waste. It's good for the planet, and you can feel good about making sustainable choices.

✔ **Focus on Experiences:** Memories and moments last longer than gadgets. Spend your resources on what makes you truly happy.

✔ **And here's an underrated perk:** Less stuff = less that can be stolen. (Bonus: It also makes moving way easier!)

DECLUTTER, SIMPLIFY, BREATHE

Too much stuff? Totally get it! Regular decluttering is key to keeping your space (and your mind) from becoming overwhelmed.

Set a decluttering schedule. Once a week, once a month, once a quarter — whatever works for you. Add it to your calendar with a reminder.

Donate or give away. Places like Goodwill or local charities will gladly take the extra things you don't need.

Think like a backpacker. Every now and then, try living with just the essentials — whether it's traveling with a carry-on or spending a weekend camping. It's amazing how little you really need to be happy.

THE GOLDEN RULES OF BORROWING

Borrowing is a great way to avoid buying. But here's the deal: *Return it in a better condition than when you got it.* Clean it, repair it, or replace it if needed. Yes, even if the lender says, "Don't worry about it." Even your most laid back friend will remember how you treated their things, and respecting their stuff shows respect for them.

Be thoughtful about what you lend.

Only loan out your own things — not your roommate's or your family's shared items. If it's not yours, don't hand it out!

When loaning something, be clear about your expectations.

It's okay to say, "I'll need this back by next Tuesday," or "Please take good care of it." Communication keeps things friendly and avoids awkward moments.

PRO TIP

Write a quick note in your calendar of what you lent, when you lent it, and to whom so you can remember to get it back before you actually need it.

PRO TIP

After using a cooler, scrub it out and let it dry completely. If you skip this step, mold will grow faster than you can say, "Ew!" To make matters worse, some stains are permanent. (When preparing for the party, you hardly ever have time for an unforeseen cleaning of the cooler.)

ADDITIONAL TIPS FOR MASTERING YOUR STUFF

Label it, love it. Invest in a small label maker (or some good old-fashioned masking tape and a Sharpie). Label cords, storage boxes, and anything you might forget about later. You'll thank yourself when you're not digging through a mystery box of cables trying to find your phone charger. And roommates will know what is yours.

Adopt the "one in, one out" rule. For every new thing you bring into your space, remove one old thing. It keeps clutter from spiraling out of control and helps you prioritize what you truly value.

Fix it before you replace it. Ripped jeans? Broken lamp? Before tossing it, see if you can repair it. You'll save money and learn useful skills. Plus, there's something satisfying about fixing things yourself.

Create a "maybe" box. Not sure whether to part with something? Toss it in a "maybe" box. If you haven't used or missed it after six months, it's probably time to let it go.

Perform a digital declutter. Your physical stuff isn't the only thing that can pile up. Take time to organize your digital life — delete unused apps, unsubscribe from junk emails, and back up your important files. A tidy computer desktop can be just as refreshing as a clean room.

Keep an "essentials kit" ready. Make a small kit of items you always seem to need: scissors, tape, a flashlight, batteries, safety pins, a sewing kit, and a multitool. When dealing with minor emergencies, it is your go-to stash.

Rent or share big-ticket items. Why buy a steam cleaner, power drill, or waffle maker if you'll only use it once a year? Many neighborhoods have rental options or community-sharing programs. Bonus: Less stuff to store! City libraries often have a tool lending program where you can borrow tools the same way you borrow books.

Make storage functional and fun. Use colorful bins, wall hooks, or creative shelving to keep things organized in a way that makes you happy and is pleasing to look at. When storage is both practical and visually appealing, it's easier to stick to good habits.

Keep the things that spark joy (really). Take a page from Marie Kondo's book *The Life-Changing Magic of Tidying Up*. If it doesn't bring you joy or serve a clear purpose, it might be time to say goodbye. Sentimental items can be tricky, so limit yourself to a small box of meaningful mementos.

Inventory your valuables. For your pricier possessions (laptops, jewelry, bikes, etc.), take photos and jot down serial numbers. Store this info in a safe place in case something gets lost or stolen.

Use deep or paid storage as a stopgap, not a solution If you're tempted to shove stuff into storage units or closets you never open, ask yourself: Why am I keeping this? Storage is for short-term overflow. Are you hiding things as an excuse to avoid decision-making about them?

WRAP UP!

Your things are there to serve you — not the other way around.

Keep what you need, let go of what you don't, and take care of what you have. Yes, dealing with your things takes time and effort, but when decluttering and maintenance are tackled on a regular basis, life is better.

For a declutter calendar and more thoughts on "stuff," go to UnsolicitedAdviceBooks.com.

Your CAR

Your Car = FREEDOM.

But it also = RESPONSIBILITY. Decide if you really need a car where you're living. The cost of parking, gas, maintenance, and insurance can add up fast. Read on for tips to keep your ride in shape.

Got a big car (van, truck, SUV)? Be ready for people to ask you to help move their stuff — or them. It's okay to say no. It's also an opportunity to get to know people and to help others. It's up to you. You also don't have to let anyone else drive your car unless you're comfortable (and your insurance is cool with it). It's okay to ask for gas money. Gas is frickin' expensive!

KEEP YOUR CAR IN GOOD SHAPE

Here's how to keep your car in good shape without being a mechanic:

✔ **Car Manual:** Read your owner's manual. It's not as boring as it sounds — it tells you when to change oil, what warning lights mean, and all the fun features your car has. Give yourself a tour of your own car as you read it. You'll probably remember it better.

✔ **Oil Changes:** Essential for cars with combustion engines. Follow the manual's schedule, and don't skip! An oil change is way cheaper than a new engine.

✔ **Check Fluids:** Coolant, brake fluid, windshield washer fluid — don't let them run low. Your manual will guide you.

✔ **Tires Matter:** Keep them properly inflated (keep a $2 tire gauge in your car) and check for wear. Better tires = safer driving and better gas mileage. Blowouts at high speeds are seriously dangerous! The PSI listed on the tires is the maximum, so for properly inflated tires, dial it back 5–10 lbs. (11,000 accidents a year in the U.S. are due to tire malfunctions.)

✔ **Wipers & Fluid:** Change blades when they're streaky, and always keep washer fluid topped off. (Squeaky, dry blades are the worst!)

✔ **Keep It Clean:** Wash and vacuum your car occasionally. A clean car = a happier you.

PRO TIP

Always have your registration and insurance in the glove box. Keep them current! The law requires you to have them in your car at all times. And if they're in the glove box, you can always find them.

Protect your registration sticker from theft. After applying it to your plate, slice the sticker with a sharp knife or razor blade in vertical or diagonal cuts. (If someone tries to peel off the sticker, it will come off in pieces, making it useless to steal.)

Get pulled over? Stay calm and polite. Avoid making excuses while telling your story. If it's a minor offense, ask for a warning.

Don't put stuff (like your phone) on the roof of your car. You might drive off without it!

Here's what to do after an accident. First, make sure you, your passengers, and the people in the other car are okay. Then take photos of the damage, the other driver's license, car license plate, and their insurance info. If they are not cooperating or something feels off, immediately call the police for an official report.

PRO TIP

Keep a GAS MONEY jar or envelope in your car (in plain sight). This will encourage your friends to cough up some dough if you're chauffeuring them to the grocery store a lot or taking them home on school breaks. You could even add a label to your glove box: Donate Gas Money Here!

SMART ADD-ONS FOR YOUR CAR

Jumper Cables: You'll save the day — for yourself or someone else.

Napkins & Water: Spills, foggy windshields, need to blow your nose, stash old gum, or thirsty passengers? Covered.

Snow Chains (for Mountain Trips): Even with 4WD, big storms happen, and they can be required on ALL cars. Be ready.

Basic Tools: A cheap tire gauge, roadside flares, and a small first-aid kit can literally be lifesavers!

SOME PARKING WISDOM

Pay for extra time at the meter. It's cheaper than a ticket.

Don't park somewhere that's "probably okay." If you're unsure, find a legal spot — it's worth it.

Your car doesn't need to be fancy — it just needs to get you there and back safely. Treat it well, and it'll do the same for you.

Don't text and drive. Ever. Seriously. One glance can change your life. Use voice commands or pull over. It's not worth the risk.

Don't wait until your tank's on E. Especially at night, in unfamiliar areas, or unexpected traffic jams. Fill up around ¼ tank to avoid stress (and walking).

I have a bumper sticker that says, "Honk if you think I'm sexy" …

When I'm feeling down, I just sit at green lights until I feel good about myself.

For a handy car check-up check list and more car care tips and suggestions, and even some fun swag, go to UnsolicitedAdviceBooks.com.

Your BIKE

Riding a bike isn't just good for your commute.

It's a healthy alternative to driving and a fun way to get exercise. Plus, it's better for the planet — so you're basically a hero every time you ride! Here are some ideas for keeping your wheels turning and making them shine.

Safety comes first.

Invest in your safety — starting with a helmet that fits properly. And don't forget a bell or horn to let pedestrians and other cyclists know you're coming. If you're riding at night, make sure your bike has front and rear lights, plus reflectors on the front, rear, pedals, and wheels. Being seen on the road is healthier and cool!

Get a good lock.

Bike theft can be a problem on some college campuses and in cities. Look for locks that resist picking, drilling, and cutting. Go for hardened steel or high-strength materials — something that even bolt cutters would have trouble with. Just be sure to balance security with portability.

Try a U-lock (not just a cable lock – those get snipped fast). Lock both the frame and front wheel to a secure bike rack or tall sign post. Take your bike seat with you if it's quick release. If possible, park in well-lit, high-traffic areas to deter thieves.

Maintain your bike. Clean your bike regularly — especially the drivetrain — check your brakes (pads and cables) and gears (derailleurs and cables), and tighten any loose bolts. Grease the chain a couple of times a year. Use bike chain lubricant (designed for bikes, not for fixing the squeaky door) or WD40 in a pinch. Keep a clean rag handy, and consider wearing latex gloves. Avoid doing this indoors. Or, if you're not into DIY, visit your local bike shop for a checkup.

Register your bike. Got an expensive bike? Get it registered with the police. That way, if it's ever stolen and later recovered, the police can return it to you. Otherwise, your ride might end up sold at auction to the highest bidder.

What's the difference between a well-dressed man on a bicycle and a poorly dressed man on a unicycle?

Attire!

Rain? No Problem! Keep a cheap rain poncho in your backpack just in case.

LEARN THE BEST ROUTES

✔ Google Maps has a **"bike route" option** — very useful!

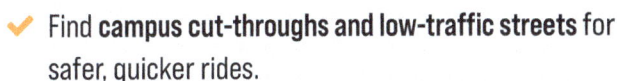

✔ Find **campus cut-throughs and low-traffic streets** for safer, quicker rides.

✔ Identify ahead of time **bike racks near where your classes are held** to avoid last-minute parking scrambles or less safe alternatives.

WANT TO MAKE YOUR BIKE AND HELMET A LITTLE MORE FUN AND UNIQUE?

For the Bike

✔ **Colorful Handlebar Tape or Grips:** Upgrade with bright, patterned, or glow-in-the-dark grips.

✔ **Spoke Beads or Lights:** Add a nostalgic touch with old-school snap-on beads or LED spoke lights for extra flair (and visibility).

✔ **Stickers & Decals:** Customize the frame with funny, artsy, or school-pride stickers.

✔ **Basket or Cargo Crate:** A quirky basket or a DIY milk crate adds both function and fun.

✔ **Fairy Lights or Reflective Tape:** Wrap some battery-powered string lights around the frame or use colorful reflective tape to stay safe and stylish.

✔ **Themed Bike Bell or Horn:** Choose a fun shape or sound — like a duck, dinosaur, or even a classic clown horn.

✔ **Custom Seat Cover:** A bright, patterned, or fuzzy cover adds personality and comfort.

✔ **Streamers or Mini Flags:** Clip some old-school streamers to the handlebars or attach a small flag to the back for extra style.

✔ **DIY Paint Job:** Spray paint a bold color or add a cool design for a one-of-a-kind look.

✔ **License Plate or Name Tag:** Personalize with a mini-nameplate or a fun message.

BIKE ETIQUETTE = NO DIRTY LOOKS

✔ **Use your bell and voice** to alert pedestrians before zooming by them. Tell them what side you are passing them on. "Passing on your right!"

✔ **Ride with traffic, not against it.** No one wants to be "that person."

✔ **Don't block sidewalks or doorways** when parking — be a considerate cyclist.

For the Helmet

✔ **Funny Stickers or Decals:** Turn your helmet into a statement piece with puns, band logos, or cool designs.

✔ **LED Strip or Glow Tape:** Makes nighttime riding safer and looks awesome.

✔ **Removable Helmet Cover:** Get one with animal ears, a mohawk, or a cool print.

✔ **DIY Paint or Sharpie Art:** Turn it into a mini-masterpiece with doodles or a galaxy paint job.

✔ **Googly Eyes or Mini-Accessories:** Attach small, lightweight decorations for extra personality.

✔ **Plush or Figurine Attachments:** Hot glue or Velcro a tiny stuffed animal, action figure, or rubber duck to the top.

✔ **Matching Theme with the Bike:** Coordinate colors, patterns, or themes for a fully personalized ride.

✔ **Faux Hawk or Spikes:** Clip-on rubber spikes or a playful wig attachment for an edgy look.

✔ **Magnetic or Velcro Attachments:** Easily switch up the decorations to match your mood.

✔ **Chalkboard Paint:** Write and change fun messages or doodles whenever you want.

Having a reliable bike provides freedom and gets you where you need to go.

For a handy bike check-up check list, more bike care tips, and bike and helmet fun, go to UnsolicitedAdviceBooks.com.

Your**SELF**

No one can take care of you better than you can.
That is, once you figure out what YOUR self-care program actually needs. The best gift you can give to the people you love is to take care of yourself. You can't pour from an empty cup, after all! Take care of yourself — physically, emotionally, and mentally. Practice self-love. Seek help when you need it. Talk through issues. And don't forget to recharge. Here are self-care ideas to consider.

Take care of business. Self-care might mean getting things done — like finally finishing that assignment or paying a bill — so you can trust yourself that you'll get things done..

Take care of your body.
Exercise. Eat well. Get enough sleep. Remember, you're worth it!

Practice mindfulness.
Try meditation, journaling, or breathing exercises to stay grounded and reduce anxiety. Try different variations until you find what works for you.

Be your own inner parent.
Picture the kind of parent you want to be someday — definitely one that loves you unconditionally. Now, listen to that parent when you need guidance.

Keep the promises you make to yourself. If you promise yourself something — like a workout or a goal — stick to it. Your subconscious will notice. (It's a fan of consistency!) But if you break promises, your subconscious will start feeding you doubt. ("Oh yeah, sure, you say it, but you are not going to do it just like last time!) On the flip side, if you follow through, your subconscious will cheer you on. ("Hey, you've been running three days a week — look at you go!") It's like having your own personal cheerleader in your head.

THERAPY IS HEALTHY

Talking things out is one of the best ways to take care of your mental health. Therapy is an investment in YOU. It's like a tune-up for your brain. A deep tissue massage for your emotions. Everyone needs a little help sometimes. Our body and brain work in tandem when it comes to our health.

How do you find a therapist? Try your college health center, ask for a referral from a friend, or search in your location at psychologytoday.com or goodtherapy.org.

If your first therapist doesn't work out, try a different one. It's important to find the right professional for you.

Try not to overcommit.

You've got a lot of freedom now, but that doesn't mean you have to fill every second with plans. Prioritize YOU first — mentally and physically. Your health comes before any busy schedule. Your body and brain will thank you for it. Practice the power of "No."

PRO TIP

Get enough sleep. Sleep is the ultimate yet strangely underrated self-care move. Most young people are chronically sleep-deprived, which can lead to mental and physical health struggles. If you are having big mood swings, it's often because you don't have enough sleep. So get your zzz's and let your brain complete the reboot it needs.

Try new things. It's healthy to step out of your comfort zone now and then to try something new you want to do.

Make time for "me" time. Protect your recharge moments. Schedule them like an important meeting. Whether it's reading, gaming, or just chilling, block out time for yourself. Don't let it get lost in the chaos of everything else. An hour a week, 20 minutes a day — whatever works for you, but make it nonnegotiable. It helps battle resentment and the feeling that you're are overscheduled.

Take regular breaks while studying or working. Use techniques like the Pomodoro Method (25 minutes of focus, 5 minutes of rest) to stay productive without burning out.

Ask for help. Life is complicated. You don't have to do it alone. Asking for help isn't a weakness — it's a strength. Think about how you feel when you help a friend. That is the feeling you gift to them when you ask them to help you. It's an honor to be asked. Just remember to say, "Thank you."

Unplug sometimes. Schedule tech-free time to read, take a walk without your phone, or enjoy a quiet moment to yourself. These days people often have trouble being without their phones. Pay attention to your level of dependency. Take time to smell the roses, listen to the breeze, and see the sky!

PRO TIP

Take a few deep breaths now and then. Oxygen to the brain helps reduce stress, anxiety, and even pain, while also improving focus, sleep quality, and overall well-being. Try it a couple times a day for five minutes.

Build your community. Join clubs, attend campus events, or participate in study groups to create a support network of friends and peers.

My brain told me I was an over-thinker ... But I'm not sure if that's true... or is it?

Limit toxic relationships. Focus on connections that are positive and uplifting. Surround yourself with people who respect and support you. Do you feel better after hanging out with this person or worse? More energized or deflated?

Stay connected. Call family or old friends regularly. They can be a comforting anchor when college life gets hectic.

Celebrate wins. Take time to acknowledge your wins, no matter how small. Finished a paper? Survived a tough week? Reward yourself!

Find your "happy place." Whether it's a cozy spot in the library, a quiet park, or your dorm room, have a space where you feel relaxed and recharged.

Engage in creative hobbies. Pursue creative outlets like music, art, writing, skateboarding, or even baking. Such activities can be powerful stress relievers.

Create some structure. Now that you're in charge of your life, it's time to create your own routines. No more parent schedules. No more school bells. This is your life, and you're the one holding the map. It's easy to get lost or feel isolated with all the new freedom, so having even a little structure can help keep you grounded and keep track of your new life.

NOT SURE HOW?

YOU CAN USE YOUR SMARTPHONE TO HELP YOU STRUCTURE YOUR LIFE.

For Tasks and To-Do Lists Use REMINDERS: Create lists, set due dates, and get notifications for tasks.

For Scheduling Use CALENDAR: Schedule events, set alerts — these are key! — and sync with other calendars (Google, Outlook, etc.); this includes your college's calendar, as well as clubs and organizations.

For Lists and Organization Use NOTES: Take notes, create checklists, scan documents, and organize with folders. You can share notes with others, like a shopping list.

For Time Management & Focus Use CLOCK: Set alarms and timers, and use the bedtime feature for sleep tracking. With Focus Mode (in Settings), you can customize notifications to minimize distractions for work or sleep.

For File Storage & Document Organization Use FILES: Organize and access documents stored on your device, iCloud, or other services like Google Drive or Dropbox. With Safari Reading List, you can save articles and webpages to read later.

For Finance & Budgeting Use WALLET: Store and manage credit/debit cards, transit passes, and event tickets.

For Health & Wellness Use HEALTH to track sleep, activity, and wellness habits. Use FITNESS to monitor workouts and movement goals (especially with an Apple Watch).

Choose routines to keep you grounded. Find a few things you can do every day to stay on track. They don't have to be big; they just need to be yours. Brush your teeth for exactly two minutes every morning and night. Have a study time and place. Go for a run in the morning or hit yoga in the afternoon. Small, consistent habits can really help you stay connected to yourself, especially when everything else feels like it's changing.

It's OK to freak out. Let's be honest — there will be times when you feel totally freaked out. You're keeping your own schedule and space while making decisions on your own, and that can be a bit overwhelming. Take a deep breath. Process and focus on the next task in front of you. And don't be afraid to make mistakes. That's how you learn to make better decisions for YOU.

Push through the newness. The first few weeks of any transition can be the hardest. You might face homesickness and confusion. But these feelings will pass. Keep moving through it. You're building your new life, step by step. There's not just one way to do this. You can explore different paths — if they don't feel right for you, change paths.

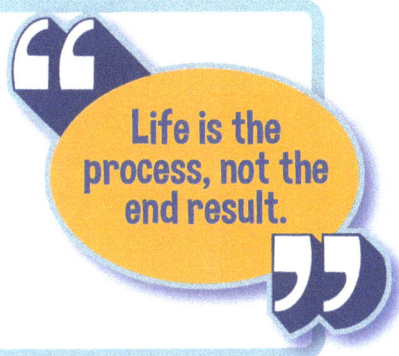

Life is the process, not the end result.

Embrace change. People will change. Technology will change. The world around us will change. And you'll change. Your interests and perspectives may shift. And that's OK. Growth never stops. Stay open, and don't be afraid to move toward what feels true to you and what brings you a greater measure of confidence and contentment.

Yes, personal change is possible. It's important to remember that if you don't like how you think, operate, or behave, you can change. No one's stuck in the same mental state forever!

Recognize self-judgment. Feelings are simply feelings. Not good or bad. We're the ones that label them. Becoming aware of your own internal put-downs takes practice. But it's worth it. Every once in a while, stop to reflect: Am I being mean to myself? Overly critical? Then, consciously coach yourself to love and forgive and laugh at yourself instead. A good test: Would you talk to a friend the way you are talking to yourself?

Recognize others' judgment as discomfort. Someone might tell you, "Why are you angry? You shouldn't be angry about that!" But really, that's more about their discomfort with those emotions than anything else. Everyone has a history. You feel what you feel, and that's okay. It's just important not to project your feelings on other people or take them out on someone else. Any satisfaction from that is temporary.

Sometimes, we lose our cool. If you do and take your feelings out on someone else, take time for self-reflection, but not punishment. Sit with the emotion, name it, be patient as you figure out your trigger. If warranted, make a sincere apology and give the other person time to heal.

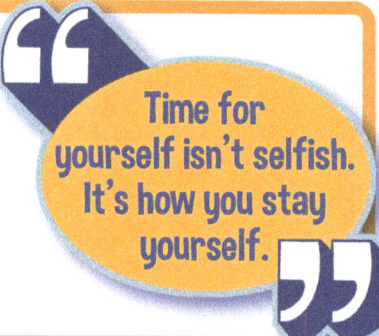

Time for yourself isn't selfish. It's how you stay yourself.

Own your happiness. You are in charge of your happiness. No one else is responsible for it. If you're always looking for others to make you happy, you might be missing out on what's already inside you. Trust yourself. Learn to be comfortable with who you are because a lot of your college and young adult experience will be about figuring out who you are and what you want.

WRAP UP!

Own who you are. That means embracing your strengths, forgiving your flaws, and stepping boldly into the world as your true self — because no one else can live your story. Take care of the only body and mind you've got. You're worth it!

For more self-care tips, including preparation for a breakup, self-care products, literature, meditation ideas, and more, go to UnsolicitedAdviceBooks.com.

Your BODY

Your body is the only one you've got.

We can be pretty harsh on ourselves, overly critical about different parts of our bodies. It's important to embrace the body you have. Here are some reminders for valuing and taking care of the temple that is your body.

Youth is beautiful. It's true. You may have heard the old adage: "Youth is wasted on the young." This is partly wistful envy and partly because the young rarely notice the beauty of their youth.

Your body talks—pay attention. Headaches, mood swings, and low energy are often whispers that you're low on sleep, hydration, or actual food.

Water is a superpower. Drink a glass first thing when you wake up. It wakes up your brain, helps digestion, and even makes your skin less cranky. Stay hydrated during the day.

Don't trust what the media says is beautiful. Yes, supermodels look fabulous. But a very small part of the population has that body type and look, so it's odd to set that as the standard for beauty. All body types can be beautiful!

Beauty comes from within.

It may sound like something your grandma would say, but it's true. When you feel good inside, it shows on the outside, and you tend to take better care of yourself, too.

Take screen breaks. Give your

eyes a break from laptops and phones by following the 20-20-20 rule: every 20 minutes, look at something 20 feet away for 20 seconds. Stretch and relax your neck several times a day. Your neck needs a break from the phone too.

Protect your skin. Wear

sunscreen every day. Yes, every day. Don't worry; you can still tan! Don't forget your neck — those areas will thank you when you're forty-five. The earth's ozone is much thinner now than when your parents were young. The sun is much stronger and more dangerous for unprotected skin. Skin cancer has risen sharply in the last ten years.

Stay away from nicotine. Addiction experts (and many addicts

themselves) agree that nicotine is one of the hardest habits to kick. (Worse than heroin because it's got similar cravings and is so easy to get and ingest.) Don't start using nicotine in any form. It's not worth it!

Move daily. Find a physical activity you enjoy — whether it's walking, yoga,

cycling, or intramural sports — and aim for at least 30 minutes a day.

Eat nutritiously. Stock up on affordable, healthy snacks like

nuts, fruit, and yogurt, and aim for balanced meals whenever possible. Keep a water bottle handy to stay hydrated. A regular healthy diet gives you the freedom to junk out once in a while with fewer consequences.

ESSENTIAL DAILY STRETCHES FOR A HAPPIER BODY!

These take 5 minutes or less, require zero equipment, and help you feel less like a pretzel and more like a functioning human.

1. Neck Roll + Shoulder Shrug

Relieves tech neck and tension from stress or screen time.
– Slowly roll your head in circles. Shrug and release shoulders 10x.

2. Cat-Cow Stretch (on hands and knees)

Wakes up your spine and improves posture.
– Arch and round your back slowly, syncing with your breath.

3. Forward Fold (Standing or Seated)

Stretches hamstrings and releases lower back tension.
– Let your upper body hang. Bend knees if needed.

4. Seated Spinal Twist

Great for digestion and spinal health after long periods of sitting.
– Sit tall, twist gently to one side, hold for 20–30 seconds, then switch.

5. Calf Stretch Against a Wall

For anyone who walks, runs, stands, or wears shoes.
– Step one foot back, press heel down. Switch sides after 30 seconds.

Don't skip preventative care. Schedule regular check-ups and dental appointments, and get your yearly flu shot and updated COVID-19 boosters. Campus health centers can often provide affordable care.

Create your circle of care providers. Find out how to use your college's health center. Learn how to use your health insurance to find a doctor in your new location. Message your existing doctor to ask questions whenever they arise. Know where the local hospital is, just in case. You're now in charge of your health. A little initial navigation will save you from stress if you get sick or injured.

Laugh often. Watch a funny show, listen to a comedy podcast, or share jokes with friends — laughter really is good medicine!

Clean hands often. Carry a small bottle of hand sanitizer in your backpack or purse.

LOL

The plague, the flu, and the common cold walk into the room. I asked, "What is this? Some kind of sick joke?"

WRAP UP!

Take good care of your body. Loving it leads to numerous benefits, including improved physical and mental health, increased self-esteem, better relationships, and a greater chance at happiness. You're young. Neglecting your body will make you feel old before your time.

For a handy list of body care tips and more, go to UnsolicitedAdviceBooks.com.

Your FEET

A separate section on your feet?

Yes. Taking care of your feet is crucial because they are the foundation of your body, supporting your weight and enabling movement. Neglecting them with poor shoes and too much pressure can lead to pain, mobility issues, and even complications in other parts of the body. Healthy feet contribute to overall comfort and well-being. Check it out!

Buy good shoes. One good pair of shoes is worth ten pairs of cheap, uncomfortable ones that you buy because they look good or were on sale. Your feet withstand more pressure each day than any other part of your body. Find shoes that fit well and last long, and your feet and joints will stand the test of time. (pun intended!)

Let your shoes breathe. Damp shoes + no air = some serious stank. Rotate pairs so they dry out, and go barefoot or wear clean socks at home (skip that in the dorm shower). Stuff them with newspaper or dryer sheets overnight to fight funk.

Trim your toenails straight across. Curving them can lead to ingrown toenails, which sound minor until they become the tiny tyrants of your life.

Sock game matters. Change them daily. Choose moisture-wicking if you're on your feet a lot. Cotton is fine, but sweaty feet need a fabric that fights back.

Choose the right shoe for the job. Wearing the right shoes for your activity isn't just about comfort — it's about safety and performance. Running shoes provide the cushioning and support your feet need to absorb impact, while hiking boots offer stability and grip on uneven trails. Using the wrong shoes can lead to discomfort, blisters, or even injuries. So, whether you're hitting the gym, the trails, or the dance floor, invest in the right footwear to keep your feet happy and your goals within reach! (Try not to play basketball or lift weights in flip flops.)

On a tight budget? If you can't afford a variety of specialized shoes, invest in a good pair of all-purpose athletic shoes and customize them with inserts. Gel or foam insoles can provide extra cushioning for running, while arch-support inserts can improve stability for hiking or long walks. Another trick is to select shoes that have detachable insoles so you can change them out according to your activities as needed. While it's not perfect for every sport, this approach can stretch your budget and keep your feet supported! You can also search second-hand and thrift options, look for online deals and discount sites (just make sure they're legitimate), and consider budget-friendly shoe retailers and outlets.

Protect and moisturize your feet now and then. Especially if you walk barefoot or in flip flops a lot, soles can crack. Dry, cracked, or painful feet can significantly impact your daily activities and quality of life. Soak your feet in warm water, pat dry, and add lotion. Apply a topical antibiotic ointment to cracks and bandage them to avoid infection.

LOL

What kind of shoes does Captain Hook hate?

Crocs!

Athlete's Foot is normal and easy to treat. Are your feet starting to smell and cracking between the toes? Apply an over-the-counter antifungal cream to dry, clean feet before putting socks on, twice a day. It'll usually be gone within days, but if you've had it for a while, it could take a couple weeks. To avoid fungus-feet, keep your paws clean and dry, wear breathable shoes and socks, and change shoes and socks regularly.

What kind of jokes do shoelaces tell?

Knot-knot jokes!

Dog poop incident? How to deal with it. If you step in dog poop, don't just scrape it off on the grass or curb. Go to a sink, wash it off, and scrub those treads clean. You don't want that lingering smell around your house!

Feet need TLC. Foot rubs with a romantic partner are a sweet, caring gesture. Keep some nice-smelling foot lotion around. Your feet will appreciate the care (and the lotion). Also, dry splits feel like hell, are easily infected, and take forever to heal.

WRAP UP!

Taking good care of your feet offers a lot of advantages, including preventing injuries, maintaining mobility, and ensuring a comfortable and active daily life. Besides, your feet will be ready for both massages and public display!

We have more afoot for foot care at UnsolicitedAdviceBooks.com.

Your ROOMMATES

Living with others is about communication, consideration, and consistency.

Adjusting takes time. Feeling at home doesn't happen overnight. Be patient — it's normal to take time to get to know people and settle in. You may feel weird and unsettled for a while. It will pass. Read on for ways to up your roommate game.

COMMUNICATION

Communication is key. Roommates come with their own habits and quirks. Here are some ways to start off strong.

Talk early (before things get weird).
Discuss living preferences, cleaning, quiet hours, guests, and more, before you end up in a passive-aggressive sticky note war.

Clean Much?

Set boundaries.
Respect each other's space, belongings, and differences. Decide what is okay to share and what isn't. Don't borrow without asking.

Maintain roommate relationships.
Set a time for regular roommate hangouts, a dinner, a movie, a game night, or a dessert together. You'll stay acquainted and be more likely to respect each other, even if you have differences.

PRO TIP

Use the "I" statement.
It works! Let's talk about the "I" statement — it's kind of like the superhero of communication. When you're in conflict or talking about feelings with a friend, partner, or roommate, the person will hear you better if you say, "I feel disrespected when ..." rather than "You disrespect me when you..." The first one is about you; the second one is an accusation that can put anyone on the defensive. The "I" statement allows you to own your emotions and reactions while giving the other person space to reflect on their words or actions. It can save friendships and romantic relationships!

Address issues calmly. Conflict isn't fun, but it's another chance to grow. Have regular roommate check-ins about rules, rent, or anything that needs to be addressed. Make it separate from hangouts. Practice "I" statements (e.g., "I feel anxious when the room is cluttered. I really need your help to keep it picked up.") to avoid blame.

My pot-smoking college roommate decided to choose theology as his major.

He's now a high priest.

Your safety matters. Your home should always feel safe and comfortable; if it doesn't, speak up! Talk to your Resident Advisor (RA), campus Housing Director, or a trusted friend or family member. You don't have to stay in a situation that feels unsafe or miserable.

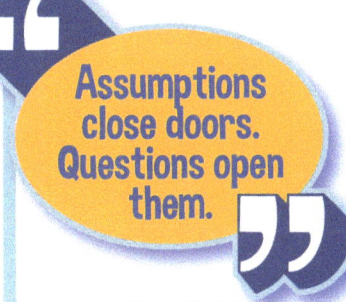

Assumptions close doors. Questions open them.

Ask questions first. Rather than assume you know what happened, ask questions first. This sounds simple, but it's powerful! You'll learn more about the situation and be able to address it better and with less bias and anger. And the person you are talking to will feel heard and be more likely to work with you toward a solution.

Try open-ended questions.
Asking the right questions can really change a conversation. Instead of the yes/no questions that might make you sound like an investigator, try something open-ended: "What's been on your mind today?" or "How do you feel about that?"

CONSIDERATION

Consideration counts. Clean up after yourself, don't hog shared spaces, and be mindful of noise and schedules.

A huge part of being a good roommate is regularly picking up and putting away your stuff! Inside and out, if you have a yard. (Jackets, dishes, empty cans, underwear, surfboards, skis, backpacks, wetsuits, you name it). Take responsibility for maintaining the space.

Collaborate. Divide chores fairly, check in regularly, and celebrate small wins — like finally agreeing on the thermostat setting.

Notice and compliment the good stuff. When your roommates pick up or cleans, let them know you noticed. It's nice to be acknowledged, and it encourages repeat performances!

Know your neighbors. They could be future friends or lifesavers when you lock yourself out, or you need to borrow an egg, or you have a party that gets too loud.

Make an effort to be friendly. You don't have to be best friends, but a little kindness goes a long way in making your living situation enjoyable.

Your roommate has a history. And so do you. And you both bring them to your new living situation. Everyone has a past that's been shaped by their family, experiences, and personal quirks for a long time. They've got their own way of doing things — like sorting laundry, making beds (or not), or even cutting oranges. (Yep, oranges. It's a thing.)

People's reactions are shaped by their history.

Know thyself. Over time, you'll need to decide if you can live with your roommate's quirks, want to compromise, or need to change things up. How do you decide? By getting to know yourself better — your reactions, your boundaries, and your personal necessities for self-care. Then, use "I" statements and questions to start the conversation.

CONSISTENCY

Consistency matters. When it comes to roommates, small, steady actions build big trust—and help keep the peace.

Learn to recognize passive aggressiveness and don't go there. If something bothers you, address it directly and kindly. Saying, "Hey, I've noticed the sink's been filling up—would you be open to us both trying to keep it clear? It really helps me feel less stressed in the space," is way better than leaving a note that says, "Wow, I guess we just live like this now." Clear, respectful communication keeps the roommate-vibes peaceful.

Don't borrow your roommate's stuff without asking. Yes, even a phone charger. Roommate trust is a fragile thing.

Consistency = respect. Following through—like cleaning up, paying your share, or restocking essentials—shows you're reliable and considerate.

LIFE HACKS!

- **Anchor tasks to habits.** Wipe down counters right after making coffee. Do dishes while streaming your favorite show.
- **Set shared calendar reminders.** Garbage day? Bathroom deep clean? Group message reminders make it happen.
- **Automate What You Can.** Set up recurring Venmo reminders for rent/split bills. Use Amazon Subscribe & Save or a group Costco run plan for shared supplies (TP diplomacy = peace treaty).

Have a backup study space. If your roommate is binge-watching a show, having a deep phone conversation, or shotgunning beers, it's good to have another spot to go.

LOL

What makes Pokémon such terrible roommates? Some of them Pikachu!

Discuss overnight guest policies early. "Surprise! My significant other is staying over all weekend!" is not a fun surprise.

Know when to be social and when to give space. Sometimes, your roommate wants to chat; other times, they just want to stare at their laptop in peace. Learn the difference and read the cues. Or of you're not sure, just ask.

Trust your gut. If you've given it time and your living situation truly isn't right for you, seek help and advocates to find a new abode.

Step One: SHOW UP

WRAP UP!

Your roommates may end up being your lifelong friends, but they may not. Regardless, you will need to get along with them. Employing a combination of patience (communication), kindness (consideration), and clear boundaries (consistency) will serve you well.

For more roommate relationships tips, visit UnsolicitedAdviceBooks.com

Your SOCIAL LIFE

Creating a healthy social life is about finding the right balance.

It entails socializing with others while practicing self-care, taking responsibility for your actions, and maintaining personal boundaries. Your social life doesn't have to look like anyone else's. Build it around what you like to do, the people you enjoy hanging out with, and the values that matter to you. Here are some suggestions on how to shape it.

Steer clear of gossip. It might feel like social glue, but it erodes trust fast. Build your reputation on kindness and integrity instead.

You don't need to have a bunch of friends. Be friends with the people who respect you, support your values, and add positive energy to your life. It's a bonus if they make you laugh until your stomach hurts. **A good rule of thumb:** Does this person add to your energy or subtract from it? (Givers vs. takers.)

And here's the kicker – not everyone's going to like you. It's true, and that's totally fine! You'll waste a ton of energy trying to make that happen. Instead, be yourself, and you'll naturally find people who are good matches for you.

"Don't compare your behind-the-scenes to everyone else's highlight reel."

PRO TIP

If a friend needs to talk, ask, "Do you want me to just listen, or do you want suggestions?" It could save you from accidentally offering advice when they just need a sounding board.

Don't text or email when you're tired or angry. People generally don't make the best decisions when those feelings are strong.

Deal directly with criticism or put-downs. When someone disses your goals — or anything about you — remember: their comments reflect something about them, not you. Someone who doesn't have clear goals might be threatened by yours. Someone who seeks external validation might find your unique style intimidating. Show compassion for them and address it with them if necessary, but keep moving forward on YOUR path.

If it's a friend putting you down, consider using an "I" statement to express how the comment made you feel. If it's someone you don't know well, you might decide not to engage further. Or explore the relationship with boundaries intact. Beware when people hide their criticisms in jokes.

Ending romantic relationships is sometimes necessary but hard. Whether you're doing the breaking up or the one broken up with, it's difficult on both ends. Regardless of your position, give yourself a chance to grieve. It's a process. There are generally five stages:

Denial: A feeling of shock or disbelief, struggling to accept the reality of loss.

Anger: Frustration, resentment, or even blaming others for the loss.

Bargaining: Trying to regain control, often thinking about "what if" scenarios.

Depression: Deep sadness and withdrawal as the reality of the loss sets in.

Acceptance: Coming to terms with the loss and beginning to move forward.

It's important to note that grief is not linear. And you may experience other emotions, like guilt. The time required to reach acceptance varies. But just know that "This too shall pass!"

You don't have to be afraid of being alone. Leaving a relationship, even an unhealthy one, and being solo again can be tough. Just remember, to make room for a healthy relationship, you are leaving something that is unhealthy. And there are lots of ways to meet new people — through club activities, friends, online dating, and more.

A breakup is an opportunity to focus on self-care. Lean on friends or family, and find activities that bring you joy. Being alone doesn't have to mean being lonely — it can be a time of growth and self-discovery. It can also suck at the same time!

Find Your "Social Recharge" Style.
Some people need a loud party. Others need a quiet dinner with one friend and zero shoes. Know what fills your tank—and don't fake the rest.

MEETING NEW PEOPLE

Identify your values. Know what's important to you in friendships: authenticity, kindness, or mutual respect? This will help you find people who align with your vibe. This can take time.

Diversify your circle. Engaging with people from different backgrounds and interests will broaden your perspective and expose you to new ideas.

Join activities. Clubs, intramural sports, or volunteer opportunities are great ways to meet people with similar interests. Don't be afraid to try something new — shared experiences build friendships.

MAKING NEW FRIENDS

Start small. Begin with the people you see regularly — classmates, dorm neighbors, or club members. Say hello, ask about their day, or comment on something you have in common, like a class or event.

Engage authentically on social media. Adding someone on Snapchat or on Instagram is a great way to meet someone new. You can comment on their posts, reply to their stories, and send messages based on shared interests instead of generic DMs. If you seem to get along, ask to meet in person. Choose a public place and trust your instincts.

Be curious. Ask open-ended questions like, "What made you choose this major?" or "What do you like to do for fun?" People enjoy talking about themselves, and it shows you're genuinely interested.

Follow up. If you hit it off with someone, suggest hanging out: "Want to grab lunch?" or "I heard about this event; want to go together?" Taking the initiative can deepen connections.

Be yourself. Authenticity is key. Don't worry about impressing people — focus on finding those who like you for who you are.

Be patient. Friendships take time to grow. Be consistent, show up, and stay open to meeting new people.

> "Sometimes, the best friendships start with a simple, "Hey, mind if I join you?""

Be genuine and actively listen. How?

Be real. Authenticity is magnetic. People want to be around those who aren't pretending to be something they're not.

Active listening is key. Ask follow-up questions and really hear what the other person is saying.

Name-drop yourself. When you run into someone you haven't seen in a while, don't assume they remember your name. Lead with, "Hey, it's Max. Great to see you again!" and let them respond.

WANT TO DEEPEN YOUR CONNECTIONS WITH OTHERS?

Again, ask open-ended questions. After: "Did you like the concert?" Ask: "Why?"

Share vulnerably. Open up and let others do the same.

Show empathy. Put yourself in others' shoes.

Respect boundaries and keep the judgment in check. It'll do wonders for your own self-growth as well.

Remember details about the person. Refer to previous conversations. It'll show you are listening. It makes a huge difference!

Check in when you haven't seen someone for a while. Even a simple hello by text or phone will help to keep you connected. Set a date to see each other when you can.

Set Boundaries–Even With Friends. If a friend drains you, guilts you, or constantly crosses lines, it's okay to reset the relationship. Being an adult means protecting your energy.

PRO TIP

When putting a new contact in your phone, take a minute to write a couple of notes about the person to remind you the next time you meet.

SAFETY FIRST

Trust your instincts. When it comes to catching a ride or walking home late at night. If something feels off, ask for help. If something feels off, ask for help. It's okay to ask a friend to walk with you or use a safety service.

Trust your instincts about people, too. If you're not sure about someone romantically, consider waiting. If you feel lonely, call a friend instead. If it's something real, you can always exchange IGs or phone numbers and get together another time.

OF DRINKING AGE?

Getting blackout drunk is a red flag. If you can't enjoy alcohol without getting drunk every time, it's worth examining your relationship with alcohol.

Never trust an unknown source for drugs or alcohol. Even if a friend says they got it from someone they trust, ask more questions. Fentanol-laced pills and other drugs are a real danger. They can kill within 15 minutes. It doesn't take much.

Consider carrying Narcan (naloxone). It is a life-saving medication that can rapidly reverse an opioid overdose.

Never drive under the influence. There is no excuse in today's world of ride-sharing.

If someone is driving who has been drinking, don't get in their car unless you know they took the time to sober up since their last drink.

Have a designated driver. If ridesharing isn't an option, someone's got to step up.

Stay hydrated and eat. Drink water regularly and eat beforehand to avoid dehydration or intensified effects. If you are drunk and going to sleep, drink a bunch of water first, and your hangover will be less excruciating.

Pace yourself. Stick to one drink per hour and alternate with water or nonalcoholic beverages.

Never leave drinks unattended. Always keep an eye on your drink to prevent tampering.

Don't be afraid to ask for help. If someone is unresponsive, vomiting excessively, or struggling to breathe, call emergency services. You won't get in trouble for potentially saving someone's life.

> *The only way to have a friend is to be one.*
> – Ralph Waldo Emerson

BEWARE OF OBO AND FOMO!

OBO (Or Best Option): Be careful with this one! If you repeatedly cancel plans or ditch your friends for a "better" plan, it might send the message that your time together isn't a priority.

FOMO (Fear of Missing Out): Sometimes, you'll have to pick between two or more fun events or decide between studying for a midterm or going to a party. Choose one, and go all in. Focus on making the most of that experience. And if someone brags about the other event, just smile and say, "Great to hear it! Glad you had fun!!" Life is sometimes a series of decisions; not all of them pan out the way we want them to. But there will be more fun times and opportunities!

Make the First Move (Socially). Invite someone for coffee. Start a convo. Ask someone to hang out after class or work. Everyone's waiting for someone else to be brave.

> *Lots of people want to ride with you in the limo, but what you want is someone who will take the bus with you when the limo breaks down.*
> *– Oprah Winfrey*

Don't Say Yes to Everything. FOMO is real, but so is burnout. Saying "Not tonight, but let's do something soon" is healthy. Your peace is part of your social life, too.

You don't have to be afraid of being alone. Leaving a relationship, even an unhealthy one, and being solo again can be tough. Just remember, to make room for a healthy relationship, you are leaving something that is unhealthy. And there are lots of ways to meet new people — through club activities, friends, online dating, and more.

Protect the Group Chat Energy. Mute when needed. Step out if it's stressing you. Just because it's digital doesn't mean you owe it 24/7 access to your brain.

Practice the Art of Thoughtfulness. Be the one who texts "How did it go?" after someone's big day. Thoughtfulness makes friends, not just hangouts.

Have a Go-To Hangout Plan. Whether it's board games, a thrift store run, or late-night pancakes, having a "default" hangout idea removes the pressure of planning something new every time.

You Don't Have to Drink to Be Fun. If you're going out, go because you want to connect, not just because everyone's drinking. Hold a soda and dance like it's 1999 if that's your thing.

Let Friendships Evolve. Some people fade, some people become your family. Both are okay. Make room for the new without clinging too hard to the old.

WRAP UP!

Building a social life takes time and effort, so don't get discouraged by setbacks or rejections. Keep putting yourself out there, and you'll eventually find your tribe.

For more guides and resources about friendship, dating, and social life, go to UnsolicitedAdviceBooks.com.

Your ACADEMIC LIFE

If you're at college, learning is the reason you're there.

Hopefully, you'll be having a blast too, but remember to prioritize your education. It's a privilege. And you're not only building knowledge, you're honing skills as a learner, networker, and responsible adult to last you a lifetime! If you're in the workforce already, consider taking a night class or online class to keep building your skills and meet new people. It's worth it! Here are suggestions for creating a successful and manageable academic life.

Be a lifelong learner. Remain curious and continually be open to new information and skills. It will keep you young and sharp and contribute to your contentment.

Learn how you learn. As you learn new study habits and try methods of learning and getting work done, be aware of what works for you and what doesn't. Maybe even write it down. Do you like to study in complete silence? Or in a busy public space? Does it depend on the subject matter? Try everything. Remember what works.

Try not to compare yourself to others. We are all smart in different ways. One person might excel at math and have a tough time with history, and vice versa. For your required classes or the requirements of your job, you will likely have tasks that you have to work harder to master. There is NO shame in this! We all work and think differently and have unique academic and work histories.

Comparison is the death of peace and well-being.

Use the library for studying. It's quiet, peaceful, has fewer distractions, and is public, which provides some accountability. You can meet friends there and study together.

TA-hosted study groups are a must for harder classes! They know what's on the exam and will point you where you need to put your focus. STEM classes will likely have the most support and the largest number of study groups.

Create or join student study groups. You don't have to learn this stuff alone, and you can help each other.

PRO TIP

Go to office hours. Going to office hours is one of the greatest but little utilized college hacks.. It is the single easiest way to improve your grade. Meet your teachers and TAs. It will benefit you in ways you can't always predict, but it will certainly give you the inside track and set you up for recommendation letters down the road. This is where you will get helpful information for what will be on tests and will help you focus your energy when studying so you're more efficient. Plus, many of your professors will be surprisingly cool and sometimes even inspiring.

LOL

What should you do when no one laughs at your chemistry jokes?

Keep going until you get a reaction.

Stay organized. Develop a system for staying organized and keeping track of assignments, deadlines, and important documents. Using a calendar is key, whether it's a physical planner, Google Calendar, or digital app. Add important dates, manage your schedule, and prioritize tasks effectively. Seriously, you'll be so glad when you have a system! You'll be able to use it throughout your life, especially as responsibilities increase with jobs and families.

Read and review the class syllabus often. Go through it as soon as a new class begins. Add due dates to your calendar. Get an idea of the course's scope and workload. Keep that syllabus handy so there are no surprises.

PRO TIP

Try making your to-do list for each day the night before. You will wake up feeling organized and probably sleep better knowing you won't forget that important appointment or assignment.

Set an alarm when studying. If you have a ton of studying or you're feeling stuck and unproductive, try setting your phone alarm for 20 minutes, 30 minutes, or an hour and then put it where you don't see new texts or snaps. Make an agreement with yourself that if you work that entire time with no interruptions, at the alarm, you will stop and do something fun, perhaps for the same amount of time. Then, reset for the next time interval. You might try making it a little longer and build your momentum.

Boring Professor? Find a connection to the course content. The teaching styles of professors vary and, yeah, you may find yourself in a really dull or monotone lecture now and then. In that situation, it's up to you to find some interest in the subject matter to keep you going. Find a YouTube video about it, an interesting concept or a personal connection if you can.

Set up for a class project on the first day it's assigned. Even if the due date seems far in the future and you only work on it for 20 minutes on that first day, you can accurately see how much work it's going to take over the time period and plan ahead. Some steps might be more complicated than you thought. Would you rather know this at the beginning of the assignment or toward the end, with only a few days or hours left?

Pulling all-nighters studying should be avoided, but if you're going to do it, do it with friends. Those are memories you may never forget. However, all-nighters have a limited success rate since, at a certain point, your brain will stop taking in information, and sleep will help more. In general, it takes 2–3 days to recover from one all-nighter.

Coffee shops and common study areas can be a good place to study. Being surrounded by a productive environment will help you knock out your work quickly so you can get back to having fun with friends. (It's harder to waste time watching fail videos in a public cafe.)

Motivate yourself to attend class even when you're tired. Take the total tuition you are paying that quarter and divide it by the number of actual classes you have. Usually, each class is worth at least $200–$300. You've paid for it. Why skip out on what you've paid for?

When in doubt, go to class. It's tempting to skip a lecture, but sometimes it's easier (in other words, less stressful) to just go. The chances of you going back to review that lecture online like you promised yourself you would are slim. Life moves quickly.

If you decide to skip class, understand the consequences first and be ready to accept them.

Break tasks into small steps. Big assignments or goals are less overwhelming when tackled one step at a time.

Try to study a little bit each day leading up to your exams. Cramming and procrastination can lead to higher stress and anxiety during exam season. Cramming uses short-term rather than long-term memory. You will remember next to nothing just a few months later. If that is the case, why take the class?

Engage actively in your classes. Take thorough notes, participate in discussions, and ask questions when you don't understand something. Actively engaging with the material helps reinforce your learning and retention, plus it helps make the class time go by faster. This is your chance to swim in the deep end!

> *Great things are not done by impulse, but by a series of small things brought together.*
> – Vincent Van Gogh

Ask Questions Early (and Often). Confused? Curious? Ask now. Whether it's your professor or your TA or your supervisor, people respect curiosity way more than pretending you've got it all down.

Find your sources of motivation and inspiration to stay in it! Whether it's a long-term career goal, personal interest in the subject matter, or the desire to excel, remind yourself of why you're pursuing your education when you encounter challenges.

Reflect on your progress regularly and identify areas for improvement. Adapt your study strategies as needed and be open to trying new approaches that suit your unique learning style better.

Talk to your professors. TAs, and classmates! Networking can open up opportunities for collaboration, study groups, research projects, internships, and future career prospects. It's also great if you can't remember when an assignment is due.

It's okay to change majors. According to the National Center for Education Statistics, around 80 percent of college students change their major at least once during their undergraduate career. You're fortunate enough to be at a place where you can explore different interests, academic challenges, career aspirations, and discover new passions.

Study abroad. The experience builds a broader worldview, increases independence, and builds confidence. You can also immerse yourself in another language and culture, make global friendships, and have life-changing experiences. In addition, employers tend to value the adaptability, language skills, and cross-cultural experience that studying abroad brings, making you stand out in the job market. And it's an adventure!!

Get an internship. You'll get real-world experience, develop new skills, and clarify career goals. You'll also build professional connections, understand work culture, and create a potential for employment after graduation. If it's a paid internship, you can earn while you learn!

Office Hours = Gold. Professors want you to show up. Same with mentors or managers. One 15-minute chat can open doors and clear confusion you might've carried for weeks.

Find Your "Learning Zone." Are you a night owl? A morning person? Learn when and how your brain works best—and build around that.

Treat Learning Like a Job (and Your Job Like a Class). In college, treat deadlines seriously and show up like it matters. At work, take notes, ask for feedback, and learn the why, not just the how.

Don't Just Cram—Connect. Cramming might get you through the exam. But connecting ideas—through discussion, mind maps, or examples—helps you actually remember and apply what you learn.

Talk to the Smart People. Join a study group. Sit near the engaged coworkers. Surrounding yourself with people who care will level you up—quietly and consistently.

Review Before You Forget. Take 5 minutes at the end of a class or shift to jot down what you learned or what surprised you. Quick reflection = deeper retention.

Use What You Learn (Even Just a Bit). Got a new concept from a class or training? Try explaining it to a friend. Or using it in a tiny real-world way. That's where learning gets locked in.

Mistakes = Proof You're Growing. Got a B? Made a typo? Asked a "dumb" question? Welcome to the club. Mistakes are mile markers on the way to mastery. Learn. Adjust. Keep going.

WHY GO TO COLLEGE?

College can seem like a huge commitment, but here's what you really gain by getting a degree:

More Career Options: A degree opens doors to jobs that might not even consider you without one. More choices = more control over your future.

Higher Earning Potential: On average, college grads make more money over their lifetime than those without a degree.

Connections & Opportunities: College isn't just about classes; it's where you meet mentors, make friends, and build a network that can help you land internships, jobs, and cool opportunities.

Skills That Matter: Beyond book smarts, you learn problem-solving, time management, and communication skills along with practicing how to think critically — all things that help in any career (and life!).

Independence & Growth: Living on your own, making decisions, and figuring things out helps you grow into the person you want to be.

College isn't the only path to success by any means, but if you're wondering, **"Is it worth it?"** — for many people, the answer is **yes**.

LOL

Why did the sun skip college? It already has a million degrees.

WRAP UP!

When in college, there are so many activities and distractions that it's good to keep in mind why you are actually there. Enjoy the new knowledge, the skills, and the academic environment you're in. Like any people, this may be the only time in your life you get to be a full time student, you might as well make the most of it!

You can find more tips to get the most out of your education and download a guide to finding internships at UnsolicitedAdviceBooks.com.

Your MONEY

While money may not buy happiness, it can make life easier and provide opportunities.

As you step into independence, it's time to also take charge of your finances. If your guardians are covering your tuition or other expenses, consider it a rare gift. But it's still time to start solid financial habits. Down the line, you'll be so glad you did! Money affords you a better lifestyle and lets you sleep at night. Financial anxiety is the worst! It's exhausting, and it takes a toll on your health and relationships. So, let's get you set up to avoid it.

Before you head out on your own, it's time to get a checking account, savings account, and, yes, a credit card to establish your credit rating. The earlier you start, the better.

HERE'S THE PLAN

1. **Research banks and credit unions.** Compare options based on fees, balance requirements, ATM access, online features, and savings interest rates. Look for checking accounts with no monthly fees and savings accounts that offer competitive interest rates.

2. **Talk to your parents or guardians.** If they're supportive, let them have access to your accounts (with permissions). If you get into financial trouble, they can help you out before things hit your credit. If you're under twenty-one, you need a cosigner or proof of income to get a credit card.

3. **Get the documents you'll need ready.** Have your government-issued photo ID (like a driver's license or passport) and Social Security number ready. Some places might also ask for proof of your address (a utility bill or lease agreement). Don't forget to bring some cash or a check for your first deposit!

4. **Go to a local branch.** Find a branch near your hometown or school. Call the bank and make an appointment with a bank rep, ask them questions, and build a relationship. They could be your go-to for future help.

5. **Open multiple savings accounts.** Consider setting up two connected savings accounts. One should be your long-term savings — this is where you stash away money for either investment purposes or big future goals, like a car, travel, or down payment on a home. The other is short-term savings for more immediate purchases like your rent.

> **The golden rule of money management: Live within your means and make your money work for you.**

6. Open an online bank account. Make sure you're set up for online banking. This way, you can transfer funds, pay bills, and check balances from your phone or computer.

7. Use debit cards and ATMs. Once your accounts are open, you'll get your debit card. Use it wisely, and don't pay those annoying fees at privately owned ATMs like 7-Eleven or Walmart. They'll charge you to use your own money! Make sure you understand the terms.

CREDIT CARDS

Credit cards can be useful tools, but BEWARE — they're set up to make the company money and are not your friend.

Following these guidelines will help you build a strong credit profile and keep you from amassing credit card debt.

> *Credit card issuers and HELOC lenders are like fair-weather friends: They cozy up to you in good times, but when the economy heads south, they abandon you faster than Usain Bolt runs the 100 meters.*
> *- Suze Orman*

Pay on time. Set up automatic payments or at least a reminder on your phone. Don't let the interest and late fees catch you off guard. Late payments also hurt your credit score and take a long time to repair. You will need a strong credit score if you want to rent a room, buy a car, or buy a house.

Watch out for high interest rates. Credit cards often charge ridiculously high interest if you don't pay in full. You'll end up paying WAY more than you planned, so try never to carry a balance. Credit is NOT money; it's a loan at interest rates that should be illegal.

Never take cash advances. NEVER take a cash advance! The interest starts immediately, and the rates are high — like 20 to 30 percent! Cash advance totals are harder to pay off than regular principal balances, and fees pile up. It's a trap.

Remember, credit cards are designed to make money off of you, but if you use them wisely, they can help you build credit without spiraling into debt.

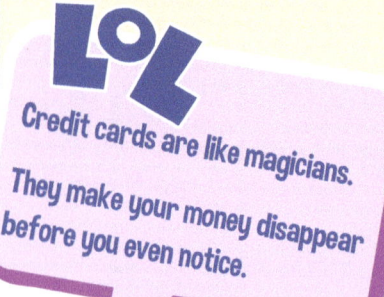

LOL

Credit cards are like magicians. They make your money disappear before you even notice.

BUDGETING, TRACKING, AND SPENDING

Create a budget. List your income (scholarships, part-time jobs, allowance) and expenses (tuition, rent, food, bills, etc.). Stay on track to avoid overspending.

Track your spending. Use apps or spreadsheets to see where your money's going. You might be surprised how quickly those small, daily expenses add up! (Beware of the daily latte at the cafe!)

Limit debt. Try to avoid too much student loan debt. A rule of thumb could be: "Don't borrow more for college than you expect to make in your first year out of school." Look for scholarships, grants, and part-time work opportunities. You can try out a community college for a year or two — it's a great way to save on tuition.

Rent textbooks. Save a ton of money by renting textbooks. If you can't rent them, buy used or digital versions. Your school library may also have copies!

Limit impulse purchases. Take a second before buying something nonessential. Do you need it, or is it just a momentary desire?

Consider working a part-time job. Consider working during college, but not during your freshman year unless you have to. There's a lot to adjust to, and you need time to focus on school and settle in. Maximize earnings in the summer and during the school year when you have a better understanding of your school-life balance.

Plan for emergencies. Set aside some money for emergencies like medical bills or car repairs. It's always better to have a safety net than scramble later.

WHY START A RETIREMENT ACCOUNT IN COLLEGE

Seriously. It may seem to early but now is the time.

The Power of Compound Interest: Starting a retirement account early gives you the advantage of compound interest. The earlier, the better. Even small contributions made early on can grow significantly over time, thanks to the power of compounding. The longer your money is invested, the more it has the potential to grow.

Establishing Good Financial Habits: Setting up a retirement account while in college helps you develop long-term financial habits and financial discipline. It encourages budgeting, saving, and thinking ahead, which are crucial skills for managing your finances after graduation. How do you think many wealthy people become wealthy in the first place?

Small Contributions Can Have Big Results: In the early years, you don't need to contribute a large percentage of your income. Even a small amount can build momentum. Starting early allows you to increase your contributions later on as your income grows.

Tax Benefits: Retirement accounts like Roth IRAs and 401(k)s offer tax benefits. Roth IRAs, for instance, allow your contributions to grow tax-free, and you won't pay taxes when you withdraw the money in retirement. Contributing to your retirement now can offer substantial tax advantages in the future.

Financial Independence: The earlier you start saving for retirement, the more financial independence you'll have when you're older. By the time you're in your thirties or forties, you could be in a strong position to retire early or pursue other goals without financial stress.

> *"Do not save what is left after spending, but spend what is left after saving."*
> *– Warren Buffett*

HOW TO START THAT ACCOUNT

DETERMINE YOUR ELIGIBILITY.

Choose the right type of account. If you're earning money from a part-time job or paid internship, consider opening a Roth IRA. It's a retirement account that lets you contribute after-tax dollars now—so your investments grow tax-free, and you can withdraw that money tax-free in retirement. It's a smart move while you're young and likely in a lower tax bracket, which means you're paying less on your contributions today and giving them decades to grow.

Check if your employer offers a 401(k). If you have a job with benefits, see if your employer offers a 401(k). Some employers offer matching contributions, which are essentially free money. Even if you can only contribute a small amount, take advantage of employer matches

OPEN AN ACCOUNT.

Start with an online platform. Many online brokerage platforms (like Vanguard, Fidelity, or Charles Schwab) make it easy to set up retirement accounts with low fees. You can open a Roth IRA with a minimum deposit and start contributing regularly.

START SMALL, BUT START.

Contribute regularly, even in small amounts. You don't have to contribute a large amount at first. Even $25 or $50 a month can add up over time. The key is consistency. Setting up automatic contributions can help you stay on track.

CHOOSE A SIMPLE INVESTMENT STRATEGY.

Consider low-cost index funds. As a student, you may not have the time or expertise to pick individual stocks. Consider investing in index funds, which track the overall market and tend to have lower fees and more stability over time. A simple, diversified portfolio will help you get started without overwhelming you. >

AVOID EARLY WITHDRAWALS.

Let the money grow. Once you've started your retirement account, resist the urge to dip into it for short-term expenses. These funds are meant for your long-term future, and withdrawing them early can result in penalties and lost growth opportunities. Consider this account 'off limits' except for deposits.

KEY TAKEAWAYS:

Start early. The sooner you start saving for retirement, the better, thanks to compound interest.

Choose the right account. A Roth IRA is a great option for students with earned income. If you have access to a 401(k) with matching contributions from your company, take full advantage of that.

Consistency is key. Even small, regular automatic contributions can make a huge difference over time.

Invest wisely. Low-cost index funds are a good place to start for beginners.

LOL

A student comes back to the dorm & finds his roommate near tears.
"What's the matter, pal?" he asked.
"I wrote home for my parents to send money so I could buy a laptop," he moaned.
"And?"
"They sent me the laptop."

WRAP UP!

Starting your retirement account now might seem early, but the earlier you begin, the more you can maximize your wealth for the future. Take control of your financial future, and you'll be thankful in years to come!

For more money tips, printable financial guides, and resume and job interview advice, visit UnsolicitedAdviceBooks.com.

CONCLUSION

The Willingness to Reflect, Change & Grow

As you step into independence, you'll likely face plenty of questions and challenges — but also exciting discoveries and moments that will have you laughing until your sides hurt.

This is a time of rapid change, where you'll learn more about yourself and the world than ever before. It can be thrilling and a little intimidating, but that's the beauty of it.

With independence comes more decisions, and let's face it, the outcomes won't always be what you expect. That's perfectly okay. It's how you grow. The key is to be kind to yourself and others, to reflect on what you can learn from each experience, and to move forward with a sense of curiosity instead of judgment.

Every failure is growth, and every misstep is a step closer to your next success. Failing = learning and is one of the keys to finding success in whatever you pursue.

Your emotions will ebb and flow — nobody's happy all the time. You will also be sad, lonely, or frustrated sometimes. However, positive attitudes are something you can choose, even on the tough days. It comes from within, and no one else is in charge of it but you. It's all about perspective.

IN OUR EXPERIENCE, THESE ARE THE ELEMENTS THAT CONTRIBUTE TO A RICH AND FULFILLING LIFE:

Love: Loving others and yourself every day.

Awareness: Being aware of yourself, others, and the world around you.

Gratitude: Finding something to be grateful for each day (write gratitude lists).

Service: Helping others and thinking about their needs.

Empathy: Understanding where other people are coming from.

Laughter: Recognizing the humor in life, even when it's tough.

Close Connections: Building relationships with family, friends, and others you hold dear; this requires vulnerability.

Learning: Be a lifelong learner, and you'll always have a purpose.

" Just believe in yourself. Even if you don't, pretend that you do, and at some point, you will.**"**
–Venus Williams

You can't make everyone happy.

You aren't tacos.

WRAP UP!

You've got more tools than you think—and you'll figure out the rest as you go. No one has it all together, but you're already taking steps most people skip. Take pride in every win, every stumble, and every lesson. Stay curious, ask for help when you need it, and trust that you're becoming the adult you want to be. You've got this!

Independence looks good on you. Enjoy the journey!

Remember, we have free downloads and even more tips on UnsolicitedAdviceBooks.com. You can even add your own tips to help others along their unique paths to independence.

ABOUT THE AUTHORS

Linda Parker Hamilton is an award-winning author, story coach, and founder of Stories to Last. She's written memoirs, outdoor guides, how-to books, and feature articles — and helps teens shine through her work as the College Essay Guru.

Doug Hamilton is a former educator turned clean energy professional with a background in teaching, public policy, and science education. He's also written about renewable energy and helped shape environmental legislation.

Linda and Doug live in Oakland, California, where they raised two sons (currently off at college), play in a band, and write books to help young people thrive as they take on the world.

Advice we wish we'd gotten:

Linda: Take care of your money. Follow your own path. Ask for help.

Doug: Understand how credit works — and how to stay out of debt.

Contributors/Acknowledgments

Amanda, Ben, Max, Kim , Cari, Alistair, Meagan, Nathan, Kelly, Donna, Adina, Michael, Chris, Ron, Don and Todd, students at UCSB, Laura and Rob, Susanne, Ian, our wonderful Stories to Last team (Anne, Kamil, Kyriaki, Arttu, Elena), and the many others with great tips who contributed to this volume.

www.ingramcontent.com/pod-product-compliance
Lightning Source LLC
Chambersburg PA
CBHW051534120626
46551CB00012B/1218